INTERACT AND ENGAGE!

 **50+**

ACTIVITIES F...
VIRTUAL TRA......,
MEETINGS, AND WEBINARS

KASSY
LABORIE

TOM
STONE

 atd PRESS

 DALE CARNEGIE® TRAINING

23   22   21   20   7   8   9   10

Adobe Connect screenshots are reprinted with permission from Adobe
Systems Incorporated.

WebEx Training Center screenshots are reprinted with permission from Cisco WebEx.

ATD Press is an internationally renowned source of insightful and practical information
on talent development, training, and professional development.

ATD Press
1640 King Street
Alexandria, VA 22314 USA

Ordering information: Books published by ATD Press can be purchased by visiting ATD's
website at www.td.org/books or by calling 800.628.2783 or 703.683.8100.

Library of Congress Control Number: 2015947320

ISBN-10: 1-56286-936-1
ISBN-13: 978-156286-936-6
e-ISBN: 978-1-60728-277-8

ATD Press Editorial Staff
Director: Kristine Luecker
Manager: Christian Green
Community of Practice Manager, Learning Technologies: Justin Brusino
Developmental Editor: Jack Harlow
Text Design: Maggie Hyde
Cover Design: Maggie Hyde and Anthony Julien

Printed by P.A. Hutchinson Company, Mayfield, PA

Contents

· ·

Foreword

I first met Kassy LaBorie while attending an ATD TechKnowledge Conference many years ago. She was listed as an industry expert in virtual training, and given my intense interest in the same topic, I knew she was someone I had to meet. While I don't recall our exact conversation, I remember leaving it with a strong impression that Kassy knew her stuff. We shared the same fundamental philosophy that virtual training doesn't have to be boring, and that online sessions can be interesting and engaging and effective all at the same time.

Kassy and I reconnected again in 2010 when she was assigned to be my producer for an ATD webcast promoting my first book, *Virtual Training Basics*. The more I got to know Kassy, the more I realized we were kindred spirits in how we thought about the live online classroom. We have since partnered on several occasions to deliver interactive online classes. Kassy has a way with people and is easily able to put online learners at ease.

In addition to her current work with Dale Carnegie Digital, Kassy's impressive credentials include working for WebEx when it was a new technology platform, and helping InSync Training grow into an impressive organization. But the most important thing to know about Kassy is her deep experience with creating interactive online sessions. She has spent most of her career interacting virtually with colleagues, co-workers, and clients around the world. She practices what she teaches, which sets the perfect foundation for writing this book.

With equal measure, Tom Stone has a storied career that intersects the fields of research and technology. Before joining Dale Carnegie Digital, Tom conducted research in the talent management arena, led product design for an e-learning company, and had deep instructional design experience for a well-known technology courseware vendor. He's also been rightly described as an "industry thought-leader."

Similar to my initial meeting with Kassy, Tom and I also met on the conference circuit. Over the years we have spent many hours in conversation about the latest technologies and industry trends. Tom is thoughtful, intentional, and mindful.

In their first book, *Interact and Engage!*, Kassy and Tom paint the picture of why engaging online sessions are important. They explain in detail the definition of virtual meetings, webcasts, and training events, in order to help readers understand the difference among them. They provide technical information about common platforms. And they offer insight into techniques for engaging remote audiences.

This book was written with the modern online workplace in mind. If you—like most—spend much of your time in online meetings or collaborating virtually with colleagues, you'll find interesting ideas for how to connect with people in this online environment. There are suggestions for interactive openings, interesting icebreakers, and thought-provoking closers. The book also includes ways to make webinars and virtual training events more engaging.

If you're just getting started with online collaboration, you'll find the first few chapters to be of particular interest. Kassy and Tom review two of the most common online platforms (Adobe Connect and WebEx Training Center), and give useful tips for how to use these tools.

The real value of this book can be found in the practical activities provided in chapters 2 through 9. These activities will help designers create interactive online sessions and help facilitators interact with their audience. Using them will keep attendees engaged. Kassy and Tom have provided step-by-step instructions for using each activity, examples for when to use them, and ideas for adapting them to unique circumstances. The book's activities are useful and relevant.

This is exactly the type of book I'd find myself reaching for when designing a virtual session. One that provides ideas that I can immediately use. It's sure to become a go-to reference guide for me, and hopefully it will become one for you, too.

Cindy Huggett, CPLP
Author, *The Virtual Training Guidebook:*
How to Design, Deliver, and Implement Live Online Learning
Raleigh, NC
September 2015

Acknowledgments

. . . .

This is the first book for Tom and me, and it couldn't have been possible without the help and support of many people, including all the online participants who have brainstormed their ideas with us over the years. Thank you for the inspiration to bring them together in this book.

When Hunter Gilliam said to me, "You do it, you're the actor. Just make it sound great, like you're on the radio!" he inspired me to make my first virtual training in 1999 engaging, rather than worrying so much about the technology. Thank you, Hunter.

Without Cindy Huggett's support, guidance, and cheerleading, this book would still be inside my head, rather than in print. Many thanks, Cindy!

Thank you to Jennifer Hofmann for giving me the freedom to creatively teach online and present ideas at conferences, while gaining years of experience. It's more than I ever dreamed of and exactly what I was hoping for at the same time!

Thank you to Nanette Miner for inspiring me to be a better trainer. Your masterful instructional design showed me how much more I could get out of training if I followed my trainer manual.

Thank you to Rich and Elaine Karakis of ExecuTrain for requiring me to learn software accurately and quickly. These are skills I still use every day.

Thanks to countless others from the industry whom I have learned from and worked with over the years: Jane Bozarth, Elizabeth Rigney, Leslie Rawlins, Jacqueline Ferras, Roger Courville, as well as the many online participants who let me test these activities on them!

Justin Brusino's patience will go down in history, because he and I began this book conversation in early 2011. Thanks to him, Jack Harlow, and the team at ATD involved in the production of this book.

While Tom and I wrote this book on weekends and evenings, we'd like to thank all of our Dale Carnegie colleagues for their support and encouragement throughout the process. Most of all, I'd like to thank Dan Heffernan, vice president and general manager of Dale Carnegie Digital, for building such a great team, giving me the opportunity to share what I know about Live Online delivery and design and to continue to grow in this exciting field.

In addition to colleagues, we'd also like to thank our family—George and Charlotte Sanford, Paul and Cathy Stone, and Wyatt LaBorie—for their patience, as we spent long hours on this book project. We know it meant less time together than we would have liked.

And finally, I'd like to thank Tom Stone for joining me on this journey as book co-author. Tom provided some of the writing, lots of editing and structure, and all the encouragement a gal could ask for.

Introduction:

Interact and Engage

. . . .

Creating outstanding online meetings, webinars, and training programs can be difficult. This is true for novice instructional designers and facilitators—and for experienced ones. It can be difficult because participants may find meetings uninteresting. They may multi-task—or worse, zone out—during webinars. In addition, online training programs may fail to produce changed behavior and improved performance.

So how can virtual facilitators captivate online participants and get them to interact and engage? With more than 50 activities ranging from openers and icebreakers to closers, this book offers the framework to ignite online events, specifically online training programs, meetings, and webinars. Accompanying the activities are backstories (sidebars) from Kassy LaBorie's years of experience that provide context for what inspired the activities.

This introduction provides brief definitions and descriptions of online training programs, meetings, and webinars. Chapter 1 then focuses on the technology platforms themselves, to explain industry terms such as *chat*, *whiteboard*, and *breakouts*. It also discusses the producer, a role critical to successful online events. Chapters 2 to 8, the meat of the book, provide examples of activities arranged by type. Naturally, welcomers and warm-ups—activities for before a live online session begins—come first (chapter 2). These are followed by icebreakers—activities for the beginning of a live online event (chapter 3). Chapters 4 to 6 provide activities specific to meetings, webinars, and training events.

Chapter 7 provides closers, and chapter 8 provides some fun activities for celebrations, such as holiday parties, good-byes, and baby showers. Chapter 9, similar to chapter 1, focuses on online platform features, but goes into more depth on some key advanced features. Chapter 10 wraps up the book and provides some concluding thoughts.

It's not a requirement to read the chapters in order, from cover to cover. Think of *Interact and Engage!* as a recipe book that cooks turn to for that dish that makes a good meal great. Virtual facilitators, producers, and instructional designers can flip through the book and jump to the chapters most appropriate to their interests and needs.

Virtual Meetings

Virtual meetings, as the term is used in this book, are much more than conference calls, with multiple people on the same audio or video call discussing strategy, a project, or other joint concern. Virtual meetings allow participants to share their screens, content slides, videos, and more. Participants can text chat with each other in addition to talking by audio. And they can collaborate on whiteboards while taking notes. Platforms for virtual meetings include GoToMeeting, Adobe Connect, WebEx, and others.

The trend toward more virtual meetings started as early as the mid-1990s, when the International Teleconferencing Association reported in 1997 that the teleconferencing industry in North America had grown 30 percent a year since 1993. And then in 1999, WebEx ran an ad campaign using the slogan, "We've got to start meeting like this!"

Now, web and video conferencing is becoming close to ubiquitous. Sixty percent of C-level executives in North America surveyed by Frost & Sullivan in 2012 said they were using web conferencing tools in their companies, while 58 percent said the same about video conferencing (Jain 2013). And the future is bright. In 2014, Meeting Professionals International found that 66 percent of respondents surveyed for its spring edition of Meetings Outlook predicted larger attendance numbers for virtual events in the near future, compared to just 53 percent for live event attendance (Meeting Professionals International 2014).

Virtual meetings increased in popularity as workforces spread out across different office locations, as travel costs rose, and as travel continues to be burdensome. In addition, more people than ever are working partly or entirely from home. The 2010 U.S. Census found that 13 million of 142 million workers spent at least one day a week working from home (about 9 percent), a notable increase from the 9.2 million of 132 million workers (about 7 percent) in the 1997 census (U.S. Census Bureau 2013). Sure, Yahoo! CEO Marissa Mayer made a splash in 2013 when she changed the company's corporate policy to force all at-home workers to instead work from Yahoo! offices. But it seems the longstanding trend of ever-increasing numbers of employees working from home will continue and perhaps accelerate as technology and management practices evolve and improve to support remote workers.

And part of that support can and should come from improving the quality and productivity of virtual meetings. Using the virtual meeting activities in this book can increase participant engagement, equaling and even surpassing that of the best in-person meetings (see chapter 4).

Webinars

Web conferencing as it is known today arose in the late 1990s, and somewhere along the line the term *webinar* became the portmanteau of web and seminar. Broadly, a webinar is a live presentation that occurs over the web. It is different than a virtual meeting, because while there can (and should) be interaction with the audience, a webinar presentation is largely in one direction: from one or more presenters to a potentially very large audience. Webinars are most commonly used in marketing—to educate potential customers about the features of a new product or service. Other webinars, more educational or "thought leadership" in nature, share information about a topic without a direct intention of selling a product or service.

This book distinguishes between a webinar and a virtual training event, primarily based on the size of the audience, because this factor determines how much the facilitator can interact with participants—and thus the ways that the facilitator can engage them through activities. Webinars have several dozen or even hundreds of participants, whereas virtual training programs are best designed for at most 20 participants. Much of engaging webinar and virtual training audiences is similar, but some activities and approaches are more effective with a smaller group.

Recently, some facilitators have started to refer to their recorded online presentations—either scripted recordings with no audience present or recordings of what were live events with an audience at a specific date and time—as webinars. In either case, the person watching the recording has no opportunity to interact with the presenter or anyone else. This changes the engagement potential drastically, reducing the audience from participants to simply viewers. These programs are thus a different concept from webinars, and so deserve a different name. This book will follow others, such as Cindy Huggett's *The Virtual Training Guidebook* (2014), and call them "webcasts," because they are so similar to broadcast television programs.

Backstory

Reasons pop up all the time that cause people to miss the interactive, engaging live webinar event they signed up for (last-minute schedule conflicts, emergencies, higher priority meetings), so they often ask me for recordings to watch after the fact. That's fine. However, there are those who think that by simply watching the recording they will get as much value as they would from attending the live event.

A recording is different in kind—it turns a webinar into a webcast. There's no opportunity to ask questions, get feedback, interact with other participants, share responses in polls, or even become more adept with the webinar platform software. As I often say, watching a webinar recording is like being a fly on the wall at a party that occurred last week.

So while sharing webinar recordings is OK, let's be clear that the value of watching it will be greatly diminished by not participating live.

Just as virtual meetings (and virtual training programs) can be executed very well or very poorly, so too can webinars be interactive and engaging—or boring lectures that quickly drive participants to multitask or, worse, snooze. But there's an antidote: well-designed activities meant for large audiences that make the most of the tools available in the webinar platform. This book provides many openers, icebreakers, and closers that can be used in webinar events, plus an entire chapter full of activities specifically designed for webinars (see chapter 5).

Virtual Classroom Training

Online training, or e-learning, comes in a few varieties and goes by many names. The learning and development industry rightfully distinguishes between that which participants perform on their own at any time and that which participants attend with an instructor (and usually other participants) at a set date and time. The first type of online training is often called "self-paced e-learning," "on-demand e-learning," or "asynchronous e-learning." Its popularity since the 1990s has been fueled by the appealing 24x7, anytime-anywhere nature of the courses; the rise of various vendors with large libraries of off-the-shelf self-paced courses; and the growth of various rapid e-learning development tools that create everything from basic voice-over PowerPoint courses, to rich animation and video courses, to more advanced simulations with branching logic. For some in the industry, this type of online training has even become synonymous with the word *e-learning*.

The second type of online training is in some ways the opposite of self-paced, individual courses. It too goes by several names, such as "virtual classroom," "virtual instructor-led training (VILT or vILT)," "synchronous online learning," and "live online training." At its essence, it is a training experience that most frequently has multiple participants and one or more facilitators (such as a trainer and a producer) together at the same time in an online classroom that allows them to communicate, interact, and collaborate with one another; view presentations, videos, or other content; and engage in large and small group learning activities.

Each type of online learning has its pros and cons (see chapter 6). And several trends have emerged from data on the use of these types relative to other forms of formal training, most notably traditional (in-person) instructor-led training (Table I-1):

TABLE I-1: SELF-PACED ONLINE TRAINING AND INSTRUCTOR-LED CLASSROOM AND ONLINE TRAINING, 2003–2013

	Instructor-Led Classroom by %	Instructor-Led Online by %	Self-Paced Online (Networked) by %
2003 (n=278)	66.01	2.92	12.66
2004 (n=246)	68.24	4.06	13.99
2006 (n=221)	65.30	4.24	19.13
2007 (n=314)	61.06	6.42	18.21
2008 (n=301)	63.69	4.81	18.27
2009 (n=304)	58.84	5.64	22.06
2010 (n=412)	59.11	6.69	18.08
2011 (n=461)	59.43	8.75	16.43
2012 (n=475)	54.28	10.33	16.96
2013 (n=340)	54.62	9.33	17.89

* Consolidated averages are based on organizations that provided relevant data for the appropriate calculations.
**Consolidated data not available for 2005 because of transition to WLP Scorecard.
***Some column titles adjusted in 2011.
****Some historical data have been revised.

- Traditional instructor-led training has been slowly declining during the past 10 years.
- Self-paced online training slowly rose. It peaked in 2009, but is now below usage levels from 2006.
- Virtual classroom training has more than tripled over the period.

The peak in use of self-paced e-learning and the slip back to 2006 levels is largely attributable to many organizations using fewer custom and off-the-shelf courses; the big off-the-shelf self-paced e-learning course providers failing to innovate and update content; and the realization that, as Dan Heffernan, vice president and general manager of Dale Carnegie Digital, once said: "People don't want to learn from software. They want to learn from people aided by software."

That sentiment is one factor driving the slow but consistent rise in interest and use of virtual classroom training programs by individuals and organizations around the world. Gathering at a set date and time in an online environment, participants can learn from and collaborate with other participants, as well as the subject matter expert facilitators, who are often the same trainers they had in the traditional, in-person classroom in years past. Other factors mirror those driving the increase use of virtual meetings: dispersed workforces, remote workers, and rising costs of travel.

The increase in virtual classroom adoption has been slow, however, because organizations were also presented with the self-paced option around the same time, and adopting two new training approaches at once was challenging. It has also taken time for bandwidth to improve to consistent levels that can support virtual classroom training at the highest quality. And traditional in-person classroom instructional designers and trainers can't just flip a switch and perform virtual classroom training well overnight. They need new skills and to focus on unfamiliar content development and delivery elements such as presenting to an unseen audience.

Whatever the reasons for this growth trend, it seems that virtual classroom training is here to stay. It will be used by more individuals as a great way to acquire the skills and knowledge needed to improve their productivity, move ahead in their careers, and enhance their personal lives. But, as with online meetings and webinars, much virtual classroom training is still not done particularly well. This was excusable in 1999 or even 2002, because the platforms were new, best practices were not easy to come by, and the focus was not on adding engaging activities. But virtual classroom training is now in its third decade. There is no excuse for boring, lecture-style live online training. (Such events might as well be called "dead online.") The activities and other tips found in this book are the remedy to poor training experiences (see chapter 6).

Engaging Through Activities

Participants in online meetings, webinars, and training events want and need them to be great experiences. But what do great experiences look like in each case? The business buzzword answer is that it's all about participant *engagement*—and for once the buzzword is on track. A great online meeting engages all participants, while still achieving the meeting's objectives. A great webinar that gets information to stick engages participants as much as possible with a large audience. And a great training event engages learners so that they retain knowledge, gain new skills, and see the desired behavior changes and performance improvements.

Engagement in live online events looks essentially the same no matter what the context: meeting, webinar, or training event. The following table makes clear the difference between an engaged "participant" and a disengaged "attendee":

Engaged Participant	Disengaged Attendee
Focused and attentive	Uninterested
Active	Passive
Enthusiastic and eager	Bored and frustrated
Spontaneous	Reactive
Curious and inquisitive	Indifferent
Ask questions	Goes through the motions
Willing	Resistant

Put another way, meeting facilitators need to stop running their online meetings like a typical marketing webinar, where they read PowerPoint slides to a large, mostly passive audience, only allowing for a few questions if there's time at the end.

Webinar facilitators need to stop assuming their webinars can serve as robust training programs. Such events have large audiences and don't allow for collaboration, hands-on or other realistic practice, expert coaching, and so on—the interactions needed for robust training to take place. Facilitators are setting participants up for disappointment and failure if they expect anything more than knowledge-level learning from large-audience webinar events.

And if training event facilitators are expecting rich training outcomes—changed behavior and improved performance—they need to design live online training in a way that enables such results. They need to limit the participants to a reasonable number (a maximum of 16 to 20); break out the audience into even smaller group activities; engage via audio, chat, and whiteboarding; and think of the event in the same way as an in-person training event.

Well-designed online activities—aligned with and in support of the event's goals—are critical to maximizing engagement and avoiding the above tendencies. They provide structure and purpose to interaction and collaboration. They keep facilitators from becoming captive to the features of the live online platform tool. Facilitators need to avoid using a poll just to break up what is otherwise a lecture-driven webinar or randomly asking a question in chat in the middle of an online training event; otherwise, they are simply falling victim to "shiny object syndrome"—the "Ooooh! Aaah! That feature is nifty. I'll use it!" response. Facilitators should not use a tool for the sake of using it. Rather, they should use it in support of the goals of the meeting, webinar, or training event.

That said, getting accustomed to the technology is the first step to knowing what is possible during online meetings, webinars, and training events. Facilitators need to learn the technology so well that they don't notice it any more—that it becomes as natural as the tools found in classrooms and conference rooms for traditional meetings and training events. Chapter 1 takes this dive into the technology, a must before getting to the fun of the actual activities presented throughout this book.

References

Huggett, C. 2014. *The Virtual Training Guidebook: How to Design, Deliver, and Implement Live Online Learning*. Alexandria, VA: ATD Press.

Jain, R. 2013. "Emerging Trends in Web and Video Conferencing—What's in Store for 2013 and Beyond." Enterprise Communications Blog, January 14. www.frost.com/c/10361/blog/blog-display.do?id=2257660.

Meeting Professionals International. 2014. Meetings Outlook, 2014 Spring Edition. Dallas, TX: Meeting Professionals International.

U.S. Census Bureau. 2013. "Working at Home Is on the Rise." Washington, DC: U.S. Department of Commerce, Economics and Statistics Administration.

1

Required for Engagement: Knowing the Live Online Platform

. . . .

The first step to engaging an online audience is to learn the delivery platform inside and out, backwards and forwards, and upside down. In fact, by not knowing the features of the online technology, facilitators and trainers have likely already lost their audience because they probably have participants on hold while they figure out how to upload the slides, share the desktop, or get the mic to work.

This chapter describes the critical features of live online platforms and breaks down what each does and how they work to support the interactive activities described in the chapters that follow. It focuses on two popular platforms—Adobe Connect and WebEx Training Center—and then concludes with a quick checklist to locate and understand similar features of other platforms. But before covering these key features, this chapter offers a few additional related tips.

What Is the Goal, and Who Is the Audience?

Always begin with the end in mind: what is the goal of the live online event? Whether a meeting, webinar, or virtual training session, when designing the overall event and its activities, think about what goal you are trying to achieve and any objectives that support it. Is the event meant to be informative, experiential, or fun—or all of the above?

In addition, consider carefully the audience and the context for the event. Do they know each other or are they complete strangers? Are they experienced leaders, peers, new hires, or the general public? Are they advanced in their understanding of the subject matter for the event, or are they relative novices? How experienced are they with the live online platform? And how much time is allotted for the event: 45 minutes to an hour? Two hours? Three or four hours with multiple breaks?

With answers to these questions, you will be well positioned to consider which features of the live online platform can be used for each part of the program. Without answers to these questions, it is easy to make mistakes such as using a feature just for the sake of it or providing a false sense of interactivity for the participants. Take the event seriously; it will be obvious which technical features to use.

TOPP Competencies for Live Online Producers

A producer who helps with delivery is critical to ensuring that the live online event is seamless. The technology requires too much attention to expect to present the content and engage the participants—and manage all the technical details and inevitable problems at the same time. If the technical details are most important, leaving the content and participant engagement as secondary concerns, the participants will log off and ask for a copy of the slides.

The producer provides a second set of hands, focusing primarily on the technology to ensure that all the features of the online platform work smoothly and as planned. Focusing on how to open the poll, highlight a point on a slide, or set up the breakout groups means the facilitator is not focusing on the participant experience intended by using each of those features. Let the producer worry about the technical details.

So what do producers do during a live online event? And do they do the same thing in a meeting as they do in a webinar or a training? Let's take a look at the four primary areas of support that a producer provides during an event. Producers are most critical in webinars and in training events, while the role is usually covered by the facilitator in all but the most complex online meetings. Here are the TOPP Competencies for Live Online Producers that we developed for Dale Carnegie Digital. TOPP stands for technical agility, on-air presence, preparation, and participant engagement. (For the TOPP Competencies for Live Online Trainers, see chapter 6.)

Talented producers have numerous traits. First, they are "technically agile"; they need to know the features of the online platform completely. A technically agile producer:

- demonstrates proficiency with platform features (feedback, chat, whiteboard, screen share, and breakouts)
- communicates clearly and succinctly with participants on how to use platform tools
- makes smooth, seamless transitions between tools as they are used for different session activities
- implements appropriate solutions and work-arounds when technical challenges occur
- responds to session technical failures quickly without affecting the flow of the session
- helps participants when they experience difficulties—and brings them up to the current point in the session
- stays up-to-date with current platforms (version changes, new features, release notes, and known issues)
- uses group instant messaging tools to seek assistance and offers it to others when they need it.

Second, producers demonstrate a level of expertise when they speak over the audio connection and are seen on the webcam. A producer with a strong "on-air presence":

- acts as a supportive partner with the facilitator during a session, creating discussions and monitoring time
- uses voice effectively to communicate with participants—and enunciates in an engaging manner, not in a dull or boring manner
- listens empathetically and continuously monitors what is going on in the session
- identifies any potential needs to help the facilitator and participants
- uses course materials and instructions designed for the producer to keep the session on track

- is webcam ready (wears professional attire, ensures proper lighting and neutral office background, and looks directly into the camera).

Third, producers are always prepared with plans and backup plans to resolve any possible disturbance. A "prepared" producer:

- uses the right equipment and computer for the platform (hard-wired Internet, landline phone, and approved headset)
- knows what to produce at the scheduled date and time—and clearly communicates any schedule changes that could affect program delivery
- downloads and reviews content in advance
- prepares the virtual room in advance, ensuring that all layouts, materials, and activity plans are in place and ready to go live
- conducts a thorough rehearsal within the platform with the facilitator well in advance of the live session
- is aware of backup plans and is prepared to implement them when needed.

And fourth, producers contribute to the overall "participant engagement." To advocate for each participant, the producer:

- helps participants focus during discussion by annotating and highlighting key points on whiteboards or slides
- uses sound judgment to enhance the program experience for participants with a balance of technical and content support
- takes problems in stride and remains calm so that the facilitator and participants do too
- provides timely and accurate responses to comments and questions from the facilitator and participants
- adds value to discussions by offering references, comments, and new ideas or examples.

A producer who masters the TOPP Competencies and manages the technical aspects of the event enables the facilitator to focus on the participants and their interactions. Working together as a team ensures that engagement is the priority and that the online event is a success.

See What the Participants See

Even the most experienced in running and supporting live online events might struggle to see the event from the participant's point of view. That is, unless they can actually see it from the participant's point of view by being simultaneously logged in as a participant on a second (or even third) computer. A savvy facilitator or producer will use this technique to:

- check for lag between the facilitator's actions (advancing a slide and rearranging screen real estate) and what participants are seeing
- help participants troubleshoot an issue they are having with the interface
- improve the program for the next time based on the live experience seen from the participant's point of view
- accurately provide directions on where participants should look, what they should see, and how the program should operate (rather than saying, "Does everyone see this?" Make a commitment to know the answer by looking at a second screen)
- present confidently and under control with the knowledge of exactly what presenting looks like to the participants.

At a minimum, a second monitor is needed to give another point of view. But to truly see and interact with a different system, use a second laptop. It could also serve as a back-up if anything goes awry with the main computer. If some participants are attending the live online event using a smartphone or tablet, consider also using one of these devices to gauge their experience.

A Note About Audio: Using Phone or Using Computer

Whether using Adobe, WebEx, or another online meeting tool, make it a priority to learn the exact setup of the audio choices. Additionally, make sure to always present from a clear connection or line, eliminate all background noise, and use a hands-free headset in order to easily interact with all the features of the online event. One of the quickest ways to lose the audience is to have poor audio quality. Don't let that happen.

Here is an audio checklist to ensure that the event's audio is engaging:

- Does the platform use teleconference, VoIP (computer audio), or both?

- If using a teleconference, is it an integrated teleconference provided by the platform?
- If using a teleconference, is it an integrated teleconference provided by a third-party teleconference provider?
  - Does this third-party integrated teleconference also work with the breakouts?
- If using a teleconference, is it a third-party, nonintegrated teleconference?
  - What are all the telephone controls that can be pressed using the telephone buttons?
  - Does this teleconference also include subconferencing for manual audio breakouts? What are the controls to initiate subconferencing?
- What are the muting and unmuting controls?
  - Is "mute on entry" available?
  - How can individual connections be muted and unmuted?
  - Can all connections be muted and unmuted? Does this also mute the facilitator?
- What are the backup plans?
  - What teleconference lines could serve as an alternate if the one that's going to be used stops working?
  - What is the plan if the VoIP stops working?

Before declaring the audio ready, don't forget one last important detail: participants almost always need help understanding how to connect to the audio. Be prepared with a slide or send them the information in advance. Have the producer ready 30 minutes early to help participants connect to the engaging sound of the event.

One challenge with learning an online platform is the amount of features available. Commonly used features are screen sharing, audio, and sometimes chat. Many people do not realize whiteboard tools are available, and even more do not realize these same whiteboard tools can be used on slides or documents that have been loaded onto the platform. The following checklists—one for Adobe Connect and one for WebEx Training Center—

walk through the features referenced in the activities in this book. Included in these check-lists is a section for each feature titled, "When to use." Pay close attention to these descriptions, because it is one thing to activate a feature, but it is entirely another to know *why* one cares to use that feature in the first place.

Adobe Connect: Critical Features

Adobe Connect is a powerful online meeting tool that can be used for virtual meetings, webinars, and training events. But the features themselves do not create engaging experiences. It is how they are used that makes the difference.

PODS

When to use: Pods are the panels that make up the layout of the online event. Choose pod types from the dropdown choices to create an interactive and engaging experience: *Share, Notes, Attendees, Video, Chat, Files, Web Links, Poll, Q&A, and Breakout Pods.*

How to activate:

1. Click *Pods* from the menu bar.
2. Choose the type of pod needed.
3. Position and resize as needed.

Note: Every pod in Adobe Connect has a *Pod Options* dropdown menu in the top right corner of the pod. Check the options for every pod used in a session to learn how each one functions. Make this your new favorite button.

FEEDBACK

When to use: The feedback tools are a simple and highly effective way to check in with participants. For example, encourage participants to click the green checkmark (Agree) if they are nodding their head in agreement by saying, "Give me a green check if . . ." or "Let's applaud your colleagues' efforts."

How to activate: Feedback is available by default. Show participants where to locate the feedback tools and request they click on the options as applicable.

CHAT

When to use: Chat is one of the main methods of communication in live online events. Use it for commentary, questions, and conversations. You will find that without much effort you can create robust *"chatversations."* You can also send links through the chat feature to quickly provide online resources to participants.

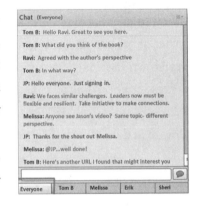

How to activate: Chat pods are included in default layouts. You can add more chat pods by clicking on *Pods > Chat > Add New Chat.* The *Everyone* chat tab is a public chat.

Note: Private chats occur when placing a mouse over a person's name in the attendee pod. They appear as separate tabs in the chat pod.

SHARE POD: WHITEBOARD

When to use: Whiteboard is actually a verb. Use the whiteboard feature for collaborative activities like brainstorming and creative thinking.

How to activate:

From a share pod, click *Share my screen.*

Click *Share whiteboard.*

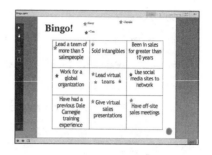

Note 1: You can also share your slides or files and then press the *Draw* button on the top of the share pod to enable "whiteboarding" on top of your prepared slides. This Bingo! example shows a slide on which participants are whiteboarding.

Note 2: You can also click *Enable Participants to draw* to allow them to collaborate and write their ideas and comments on the files shared in a share pod or on a whiteboard. To do this:

1. Enable *Draw* from the top of the share pod.
2. Click the *Share Pod Options* menu in the top right corner.
3. Click *Enable Participants to draw.*

SHARE POD: DOCUMENT SHARING

When to use: You can share documents (for example, PowerPoint files) using a share pod prepared for interaction with enough blank space for whiteboarding thoughts, ideas, and answers to questions. You can also share other types of files such as videos and PDFs.

How to activate: Share pods are included in default layouts. To add additional share pods:

1. Click *Pods > Share > Add New Share.*
2. Click *Share My Screen > Share Document > Browse My Computer* and then double click the file.

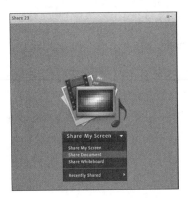 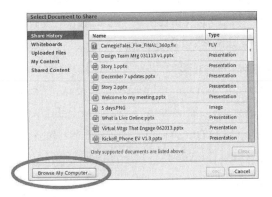

Note: See the "Share Pod: Whiteboard" feature above to allow participants to collaborate on a shared file by whiteboarding on it.

SHARE POD: SCREEN SHARING

When to use: Screen sharing has many uses, such as for reviewing a webpage as a group or for software training. You can allow participants to view your entire computer desktop, one application at a time, or just one window.

Participants do not need to have the software on their computers to view it from yours. For hands-on training, ask participants to open their own applications and toggle between the Adobe Connect window and their application as you demonstrate the steps.

How to activate:

1. From a share pod, click *Share My Screen* and choose Desktop, Applications, or Windows.
2. Click back to the Adobe Connect share pod to click *Stop Sharing* when ready.

POLLING

When to use: You can poll participants by asking one question at a time. To ask multiple questions at once, use a series of poll pods. You can also place them in their own layout if needed.

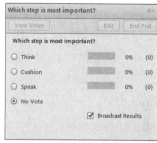

Remember to respond appropriately to the answers and build your comments and discussion into the live online experience.

How to activate: You can add a poll via a poll pod at any time:

1. Click *Pods > Poll > Add New Poll*.
2. Resize, position, and type the multiple choice, multiple answer, or short-answer question and the answer.

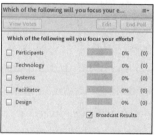

3. Click *Open*.
4. Click *Edit*, if needed.
5. Click *View Votes* to see individual attendee responses.
6. Click *Back to Poll* to see the aggregate responses.
7. Check *Broadcast Results* to the participants when necessary.
8. Click *End Poll*.

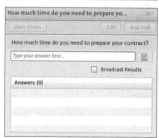

FILE SHARE

When to use: Handouts and manuals can be easily provided to participants using a files pod. Always load class materials in a files pod for quick access as needed.

How to activate:

1. Click *Pods > Files > Add New File Share*.
2. Click *Upload File* and browse to choose the file to share.
3. Participants can click on each file one at a time and then click *Download File(s)* to save them locally to their computers.

Note: Click the *Files Pod Options* menu in the top right corner (circled) for more options, such as to remove and rename files.

BREAKOUT

When to use: Working in small groups with other online participants is a great way to collaborate on a common goal or apply key learnings from a training event. Use breakouts for activities like role playing, problem-solving, and case studies where teams work together to create solutions and share ideas.

How to activate:

1. From the attendees pod, click the *Breakout Room View* button (circled).
2. Use the + button to add as many rooms as needed.
3. Click *Start Breakouts* to prepare the content for each one.
4. Mouse over your name and then mouse over the desired breakout room and prepare the activities for each (for example, add a share pod, a chat pod, or a file share pod as needed).
5. Click *End Breakouts* and return to the main room.

6. When it's time to start the breakout activities with the attendees, mouse over each attendee's name to add them to a breakout group.

7. Click *Start Breakouts* when ready for the activity and *End Breakouts* to bring everyone back to the main meeting.

Note 1: To send a Broadcast Message, click the *Attendee Pod Options* menu in the top right corner before ending breakouts.

Note 2: Your site may have a limit on the number of breakouts you can create and run at one time. Be sure to verify.

RECORDING

When to use: Recordings of the live online events provide participants with an archive of the activities for reference and review. It also helps people who arrive late or leave a session early. By being able to view the recording, they do not lose out on any of the session discussion or activities.

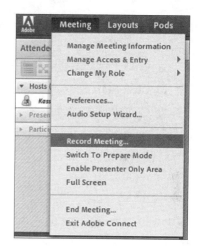

How to activate:

1. Click *Meeting > Record Meeting.*

2. Name the recording and click *OK.*

3. Click *Pause* as needed, and *Stop* when ready.

4. To access the recording link, click *Meeting > Manage Meeting Information > Recording.*

Note 1: Adobe Connect administrators must mark a recording as *Public* in order for the URL to be accessible for viewing.

Note 2: Recordings of interactive online events are not a replacement for attending the live event.

WEBCAM

When to use: You can use a webcam to personalize a live online event. It works well for introductions or for when you need to see a person or an object to reach the event's goals. It is not a best practice to have webcams turned on throughout an event just for the sake of using the technology. In some contexts it can be distracting and lessen the overall impact of the event.

How to activate:

1. Click *Pods > Video.*
2. Position the pod on the screen.
3. Click *Start My Webcam.*
4. Click *Allow.*
5. Click *Preview.*
6. Click *Start Sharing.*
7. Click *Stop My Webcam* when appropriate.

Note: Pay attention to your lighting and what is behind you that will appear on camera. Be sure your face is centered and look into the camera when speaking.

LAYOUTS

When to use: Layouts provide a custom look and feel to the live online session. By using multiple layouts, you can add variety and different levels of interactivity to the sections of the event. You can create layouts by adding pods of different sizes and placing them in different locations on the screen. You can customize and position them according to the goals and content placed in each. Think of layouts as different rooms in your house where different activities take place. Each has its own look and purpose.

How to activate:

1. Click *Layouts* from the menu bar.
2. Click *Create New Layout.*
3. Duplicate an existing layout or create a new one and name it.
4. Build the layout by selecting which pods to add to it.
5. Switch between layouts using the *Layouts* menu or the shortcuts along the right side of your Host View.

Note: To save time and create consistency, you can duplicate existing layouts. You can also hide pods you don't need.

WebEx Training Center: Critical Features

The WebEx family of tools consists of WebEx Meeting Center (used for meetings), Event Center (used for large webinars), Support Center (used for technical support), and Training Center (used for training). It is a powerful suite of platforms, each targeting a different online event experience. The features below describe those of WebEx Training Center because all three types of events—virtual meetings, webinars, and training events—discussed in this book can be delivered through it. If using one of the other centers, refer to the checklist below to walk through and see what features it has or does not have.

PARTICIPANTS PANEL

When to use: The *Participants* panel is your key to who is online, how their audio is connected, and what feedback they are providing throughout the session. Focus here more than on your slides to engage your audience.

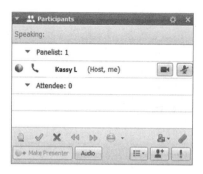

How to activate: This panel is enabled by default. You can minimize it by clicking the button in the top left corner and close it using the button in the top right corner.

Note: You will see a person's name appear first, and then either a phone or headset icon. If there is no icon, look for a participant named "call-in user." That is likely the person with no icon next to her name. This means the attendee dialed into the teleconference without referencing her attendee ID number. Ask her to enter it from the *Audio Panel* in order to connect the phone icon to her name. You'll need this so that breakout sessions run smoothly.

FEEDBACK

When to use: The feedback tools are a simple and highly effective way to check in with participants. This is your online connection to the types of nonverbal cues they give during in-person events. Encourage participants to click the green checkmark any time they are nodding their head in agreement. For example, tell them: "Give me a green check if . . ." or "Let's applaud your colleagues' efforts."

How to activate: Feedback is available by default from the bottom of the Participants panel. Show participants where to locate them and ask them to click on the options as needed. Use the feedback yourself as a way to model the type of interaction you request from participants.

CHAT

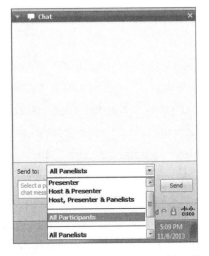

When to use: Chat is one of the main methods of communication in live online events. Do not underestimate the power of this simple tool, because it can be your main lifeline. Use it for commentary, questions, and conversations to create *"chatversations"*—conversations that occur entirely over chat. Send links through chat to quickly provide online resources to participants.

How to activate: The chat panel is included by default. The *All Participants* chat is a public chat, seen by all people in the session. You can adjust the level of chat available to participants from the attendee privileges in the *Participant* menu bar. Enable all chat options for the most effective level of interaction.

Note: You can have a private chat by clicking on the dropdown menu next to *All Participants*. Select the name of the person with whom you wish to privately chat. You will see *(privately)* an indication of who can see the chat. Also, beware of *All Attendees* chat as anyone who is a panelist will not see these messages—that is, *All Panelists* includes the host, presenter, and panelists, while *All Attendees* includes everyone except the panel.

WHITEBOARD

When to use: You can use this tool for collaborative activities in the live events such as brainstorming and creative thinking. Remember that whiteboard is a verb. Whiteboarding answers and ideas is one of the most effective ways to gauge participation levels. It not only provides immediate responses, but it is also easy to save results and refer back to them at a later time.

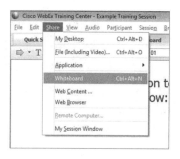

How to activate: From the *Share* menu, click *Whiteboard* to bring in a new, blank whiteboard. However, for best results create slides with enough blank space so that participants have enough room to whiteboard their ideas directly onto the slide. And then use *Share > File* to upload the slides to then be whiteboarded upon.

1. Click the *Participant* menu.
2. Click *Assign Privileges*.
3. Select *Annotate* and then click *OK*.

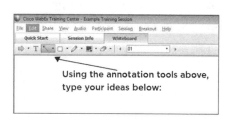

Note: Have participants place their WebEx pointers on the whiteboard space before typing a response. This will keep participants from typing over one another. We call this "claiming your real estate."

SHARE FILE (INCLUDING VIDEO)

When to use: You can share files (for example, PowerPoint files) that are prepared for interaction with enough blank space to whiteboard thoughts, ideas, and answers to questions. Participants can annotate on files for increased interaction and more-engaging activities. Try to use compelling images rather than words and ask your participants to respond using the chat, feedback, and whiteboard tools.

How to activate: Click *Share > File (Including Video) > Browse My Computer* and then double click on the file. Note the types of files recognized and compatible with WebEx by clicking on the dropdown next to *Files of type* on the bottom of the dialog box.

Note: Develop the slides to be uploaded in this way so they become the working space for the event. There is no need to share the PowerPoint application unless you need to use the application itself (such as to teach participants about PowerPoint).

SHARE DESKTOP, APPLICATION, OR WEB BROWSER

When to use: Software and systems training is often conducted live online using desktop, application, or web sharing. Participants can view the entire desktop, one application at a time, or even a webpage with the person presenting controlling the navigation. Think of it as if others are looking over your shoulder as you present from your computer.

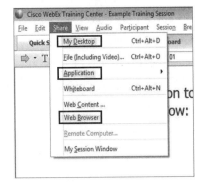

Participants do not need the software on their computers to view it from yours. For hands-on training, ask participants to open their own applications and toggle between the WebEx window and their application as you demonstrate the steps.

How to activate:

- From the *Share* menu:
    1. Click *My Desktop* to share all applications on your computer.
    2. Click *Application* to share only one application at a time.
    3. Click *Web Browser* to launch your browser and navigate to a web page or web-based application.
- Click *Stop Sharing* when ready to return.

Note: When sharing a web-based application using the share web browser feature, if the application needs to use another application that is not web based, use the share desktop feature to ensure that window is also seen by the participants. The share web browser feature only shares webpages in the browser. Also, use *Share > Web Content* to allow attendees to independently navigate a web site, rather than watch you do it. Use *Share > My Session Window* to show participants the view of your WebEx session window when teaching them how to use the WebEx features.

POLLING

When to use: You can survey participants with prepared questions and answers using polls. Create the poll files (.atp,

which for a little WebEx trivia, stands for "ActiveTouch poll") in advance and use them repeatedly in the live online sessions. WebEx poll files can include one question, or many on the same file. Poll questions can be multiple choice, multiple answer, or short answer.

Remember to respond appropriately to the answers and build your comments and discussion into the live online event experience. Do not use polling to simply get some interaction.

How to activate:

1. Preload any previously created polls on the polling panel before the session.
2. Open each poll from the *Polling* panel at any time during the session.
3. Click *Open.*
4. Click *Edit* if needed.

5. Click on the polling status boxes (which display "..." on each box) at any time to see who has not started, is in progress, or has finished the poll.

6. Click *Close Poll* and determine which results to share with participants.

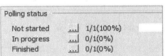

Note 1: The polling results can be saved in various formats to be used in different programs. Be sure to click *File > Save > Polling* results as needed.

Note 2: Download the WebEx Poll Questionnaire Editor from the WebEx Training Center website under *Support > Downloads.* A host login is required and the editor is found in your computer's list of programs. This will allow you to create polling files without having to first launch a live WebEx session.

FILE TRANSFER

When to use: Handouts and manuals can be easily provided to participants using *File Transfer.* Load event materials for quick access as needed.

How to activate:

1. Click *File > Transfer.*

2. Click *Share File* and browse your computer for the file to upload. Double click to add it.

3. Participants can then click on each file one at a time and then click *Download* to save them locally to their own computers.

Note: The number in the bottom right corner indicates how many participants have the file transfer window open. Ask them to close it once they have the file so you know when they are done.

WEBCAM

When to use: Using a webcam personalizes a live online event. It works well for introductions or any time that seeing a person or an object would be helpful.

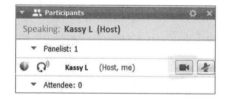

How to activate:

- Click the *Video* icon and note that it changes to green when it is sending a live feed.
- Press the *Video* icon again to turn off your camera.
- Click the *Options* button in the top right to make changes to the picture.

Note 1: Pay attention to your lighting and what is behind you that will appear on camera. Be sure your face is centered and look into the camera when speaking.

Note 2: Prepare participants ahead of time before asking them to be on a webcam. No one appreciates a surprise webcam request.

RECORDING

When to use: Recordings of your live online events provide participants with an archive of the activities for reference and review. It also helps people who arrive late or leave a session early. By watching the recording, they do not lose out on any of the session discussion or activities.

How to activate:

1. Click the *REC* panel to open the recorder.
2. Press the red button to record.
3. Click *Pause* and *Stop* as needed.
4. To access the recording link, log in as the host to your list of sessions in *My WebEx > My Training Sessions* and locate the recording.

Note 1: WebEx hosts must mark a recording *Public* in order for the URL to be accessible for viewing.

Note 2: Recordings of interactive online events are not a replacement for attending live. This is especially true for training events. A recording will not influence learning or even information retention as well as the live experience will, because it lacks interactivity. Further, many people will find recordings boring and thus will not watch for more than 10 minutes or will not be able to resist the urge to fast-forward and skip around for the parts they think are most important.

Q&A

When to use: The *Q&A* panel is used for controlling the questions the audience views. Use this feature for large online events where there is a group of people helping answer questions. Good examples are webinars for marketing and sales, or large online organizational events where publicly shared questions would not be appropriate.

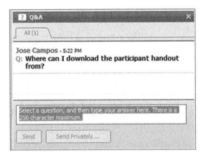

How to activate:

- Click the *Q&A* panel to open it and view the questions.
- Participants do the same and type questions in. They do not see other participants' questions until answered by a member of the panel.
- A panel member needs to select the question, type an answer, and then decide whether to click *Send* (answer publicly) or click *Send Privately* . . . (answer privately).
- Click *Send* to share the answer.
- *File > Save > Q&A* to save a record.

Note 1: Participants often get confused when they do not see other participants' questions, so be prepared to explain what is going on.

Note 2: Use the chat instead of this panel to create an open dialogue and a more interactive live online event. Use a Q&A when the environment needs to be more private or controlled.

BREAKOUT

When to use: Working in small groups with other online participants is an effective and engaging way to apply key learnings from any training event, or to split up a group in a meeting to brainstorm on one or more topics. For example, you can use breakouts for activities like role playing, problem-solving, and case studies where teams work together to create solutions and share ideas.

How to activate:

1. From the *Breakout* menu options, click on the breakout session assignment.

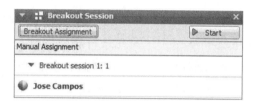

2. Click *Add Session* to add the number of sessions needed.

3. Select each participant's name and the room he needs to join and then click the *>> button* to add him to the assigned breakout room.

4. Click *OK* once all the rooms are planned. All the rooms and their assigned presenters and participants will be listed on the Breakout panel.

5. Click *Start Breakouts* when ready.

6. To join each breakout, select it and then click *Join*.

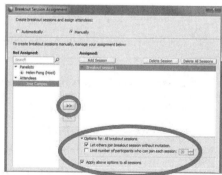

7. Leave each breakout and return to the main room.

8. Send a broadcast message from the *Breakout* menu as needed.

9. Click *End Breakouts* when ready.

10. If a whiteboard or PowerPoint slide was shared in the breakouts, request that each attendee click *Share Breakout Session Content* from the *Breakout* menu during the debriefing.

Note 1: Be sure to mark "Let others join the breakout without invitation" so that latecomers can join a breakout once it has started. They join just as you would: they choose the breakout, then click *Join*.

Note 2: Create a slide in your visuals that includes two sets of instructions for all breakout activities: activity directions and technical directions. See the example activity on the right.

Take charge! Scenarios

Instructions	How it will work
• Discuss in your small group what you will do for each of the scenarios in the space provided.	• Each room has separate audio and a whiteboard
• Take notes on the table	• We will call time alerts and call you back for debrief
• You will have ___7___ minutes to work	• If you have questions at any time, send a chat message to Host
• Pick a spokesperson to report back during debrief	

Checklist for Other Live Online Platforms

Not using Adobe Connect or WebEx? Don't worry. The other platforms for live online meetings, webinars, and training events have many of the same features. They may lack one or two features, or they may have them but are called something else. To learn the tool's features, use this list to remember the important parts for delivering online meetings, webinars, and training events. Don't let the tool determine participant engagement. How you use the features available determines whether online experiences are meaningful.

- **Breakouts.** Not all platforms have this feature. Check whether the platform does and then recheck the audio settings to ensure that they are compatible with breakouts.
- **Chat.** All platforms have this feature, but it may operate differently: some platforms allow public chatting while others do not. And some even let hosts see the private chats among participants.
- **Feedback Options or Indicators.** This is the "raise hand" or "green check" and "away" options. Every platform is different. Check who can see what and when. For example, in WebEx Meeting Center, the host and presenter can see an attendee's raised hand, but other participants cannot.
- **File Transfer.** Check whether files can be transferred and whether there is a file size limit.
- **Layouts or Views.** Check whether there are any additional "views" or "arrangements of content" that can be prepared in advance.

- **Polling.** Check whether polling is included and what question types can be created. Can the files be saved and re-used? Can the results be saved?
- **Q&A.** Check how the Q&A feature works and who presides over the questions received and answers sent back out.
- **Recording.** Check how audio is captured. Where is the recording saved or stored? Who has access to it and can it be password protected?
- **Reports.** Check whether the following reports can be created:
  - registration
  - attendance
  - recording views
  - polling results
  - attention tracking.
- **Share Desktop, Application, or Web Browser.** Most platforms have this feature. In fact, this is the persistent view for the Citrix GoToMeeting suite of products. Learn how to control when the desktop is shared and when it is not. Can it be paused?
- **Webcam.** Check whether the webcam feature shows a live feed by default. How do you control who sees your webcam and when?
- **Whiteboard.** Check how the whiteboard feature works. How do participants annotate on a whiteboard? Can your slides function as whiteboards? Can they be saved?

Conclusion

This chapter focused on the critical features of the most popular platforms, and described how they work to support the interactive activities described in the chapters that follow. Understanding these technology basics is a critical prerequisite for developing and using engaging activities. Chapters 2 through 8 of this book provide more than 50 activities you can use directly or modify and expand on to suit your needs. In each case the features used are listed, and you can refer back to this chapter as needed if you forget what a feature does or how to access it in WebEx or Adobe Connect. Now on to the fun stuff, starting with activities appropriate for the beginning of virtual events.

2

Have Them at Hello: Warm-Ups and Welcomes

As with in-person meetings or classroom training events, participants need to prepare before they use the available tools. Welcome and warm-up activities are perfect for starting an online meeting, webinar, or training event. They open the session with a purpose beyond asking participants to sit and listen. They help set the stage for interaction and collaboration. They function as early technical checks. And they help ensure an on-time start as well as a successful communication process among the participants, the producer, and the facilitator once the event starts and content-focused activities need to begin. After all, teaching participants how to use the chat feature only distracts all involved when reviewing the meeting agenda or the training objectives.

Ideally, participants will have attended a prerequisite live online session where they had in-depth, hands-on practice time with the tools before their scheduled program starts. Practice time allows the warm-up to serve as a refresher on the tools and an opportunity for the stage to be set. The feeling should be the same as when arriving early to an in-person class: choose a seat, take out the materials, log in to a computer (if necessary), and start to get to know the other participants.

The warm-up is typically conducted in the 15 to 30 minutes before the scheduled start of the session. Best managed by a producer, it usually focuses on technical aspects of the live online platform as well as the content for the training event. As participants respond to questions, use drawing tools, and verbally and textually interact, they are preparing for the event's objectives. But they are also performing technical checks: Do I know how to use the drawing tools? Do I know how to indicate agreement or disagreement to questions using the tools available? Do I know how to write and read a fast flow of chat messages? The best part is that because participants are having fun and engaging with the features and other participants, they don't even realize they are also testing their technical skills.

The producer should clearly state the intention of these activities so technical checks are in fact occurring and any issues are being resolved. As participants join the session, the producer should welcome them as they join the audio. This serves as the first test to whether their audio is working. If they do not arrive via audio within a couple minutes, the producer should send them a message through the chat feature to find out if they need assistance. The types of technical issues typically encountered at this stage most often involve participants' poor audio connection; slow Internet connection for downloading the online event software; and confusion about the chat, annotation, and feedback tools. So the producer needs to be ready to step in and solve a myriad of problems.

When participants arrive early, they are often placed on hold while a song plays in the background. Avoid doing this. Sure, everyone enjoys the sound of a great melody, but it doesn't prepare participants to be engaged in the live online meeting, webinar, or training event. By using the activities that follow in this chapter, you'll have participants warmed up and ready to succeed in the online program.

Take a Tour

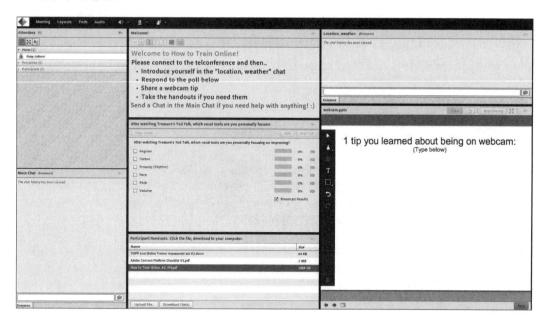

Purpose: To welcome participants to tour the online room, establishing active participation from the moment they connect.

Session format: Webinar, Training

Audience: Any

Number of participants: Unlimited

Time: 5 to 30 minutes (before scheduled start)

Materials: Slides, Handouts, Music

Features used: Polling, Share a slide, Whiteboard, Chat, File share

Description: When delivering a presentation or workshop at a conference or one on one for a client, you should arrive early and prepare the room for the event's activities. That may mean rearranging the room, hanging paper to draw or write on, setting supplies at each table, or placing a sign-in sheet by the door. You can emulate this experience in a webinar or an online training by creating a Welcome Tour. The tour may encourage casual conversation among early arriving participants—just as an in-person event would.

This allows you to get to know more about your audience and also establishes the chat feature as a normal way to talk. The tour may feature a poll question and a whiteboard activity related to the pre-event assignments sent to the participants. You can check in on their reactions and ideas and then incorporate their responses throughout the event.

Backstory

I'll admit that when I first started using Adobe Connect, I was a bit overwhelmed by the interactive choices the platform offered. Knowing this, I was certain the participants were feeling equally—and even more—overwhelmed. The idea of the "taking a tour" came to me once I learned how each of the Adobe pods really worked.

SETUP

Design needs ahead of time:
- Create a slide or a note explaining the tour and what to do.
- Design poll questions related to the topic or the pre-event assignment.
- Design a slide to whiteboard answers to a question related to the topic or pre-event assignment.
- Create handouts to use during the event.
- Think of a question for the chat.

Before the activity begins:

Facilitator: Prepare to encourage participants to "take the tour" by taking it yourself. For instance, respond to the questions so that others see a sample response.

Producer: Ensure that public chat is enabled and that whiteboard tools are enabled. Provide guidance on the tools as needed.

THE ACTIVITY

SAY	DO
Facilitator: "Welcome to our session today! Please connect your teleconference (or microphone for VoIP) and then participate in our opening activities."	*Producer:* Assist participants with their audio connections.
Facilitator: "Once you have connected your audio, take a moment to tour the room and get acquainted with the tools we will use to communicate today. Where are you located, and what did you think of the pre-event assignments? Please respond in the indicated areas."	*Facilitator:* Comment on their responses, validating their contributions and getting to know them at the same time. *Producer:* Assist participants with instructions for using the chat, the whiteboard, and any other tools.
	Facilitator: Once the event officially starts, take 30 seconds to 1 minute to summarize what occurred in the Welcome Tour for those who just arrived and missed it. This will encourage them to arrive early to your next event so they too can participate.

Make it clear that this tour was before the session so those who do arrive on time do not get upset that you "started early" and without them.

Transition after the activity:

Facilitator: "It was a pleasure getting to know you and checking in with each of you on the pre-event assignments. You have provided insights to inform our learning today. Let's get started on the topic of *[insert class topic here]*."

SPICE IT UP WITH THESE ALTERNATIVES

- For a webinar, rather than a small training group, add music using a share pod or soft music playing in the background so that people have something to listen to as they take the tour.
- Create a slide to introduce them to the tour, rather than the note pod you see in the screenshot above.
- Add pictures of the attendees if you have them, or have them sign their names on a sign-in sheet when they join.
- With a countrywide or global audience, have participants sign in by adding their location on a map.

Trivia

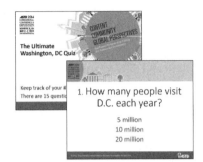

Purpose: To engage participants with a fun piece of trivia right from the start.

Session format: Meeting, Webinar, Training

Audience: Any

Number of participants: Unlimited

Time: 5 to 30 minutes (before scheduled start)

Materials: Slides

Features used: Share a slide, Chat

Description: Trivia questions are an easy, effective way to quickly engage an audience. They also are very easy to design on slides and to load into a virtual environment. Choosing trivia related to the meeting, webinar, or training event piques the interest of participants as soon as they connect. It gets them thinking about the subject early, thus helping you make the most of every minute. You can also add a layer of competition by asking that participants: "Keep track of your number of correct answers. And share it in the chat." This establishes an environment where participants are encouraged to work, share, and learn together.

SETUP

Design needs ahead of time: Create a slide deck with the questions and answers.

Before the activity begins:

Facilitator: Review the trivia and greet participants as they join, encouraging them to jump in (and keep track of their scores, if desired).

Producer: Load the slides with the trivia. Ensure that public chat is enabled.

THE ACTIVITY

SAY	DO
Facilitator: "Welcome to our session today! While we wait for the main event, take a moment to test your knowledge. Keep track of the number of answers you answer correctly and at the end share your result in the chat."	*Producer:* Help participants connect to the audio and then provide direction on using the chat if necessary. *Producer:* Set the slides to run on an automatic timer. (Most platforms allow this. If the platform doesn't, the facilitator or the producer will need to manually advance them.)
Facilitator: "So how did you do? Let's see who got the most answers correct before we start our program today."	*Producer:* Help the facilitator by quickly reviewing the chat results and verbally noting who got the most right. *Facilitator:* Review the chat and comment.

Transition after the activity:

Facilitator: "We hope you had time to enjoy the trivia and perhaps you learned something you did not know! Let's get started on the topic of *[insert class topic here]*."

SPICE IT UP WITH THESE ALTERNATIVES

- For meetings, consider using company history trivia.
- For webinars, consider using trivia about the product, industry, or company that you are presenting about.
- For training events, gather information about the participants in advance and create questions about them. Or ask questions about the prerequisite knowledge for the program—but keep it fun.

Pumpkin Carving

Purpose: To engage participants by using the white-board's drawing tools.

Session format: Meeting, Training

Audience: Any

Number of participants: Unlimited

Time: 5 to 30 minutes (before scheduled start)

Materials: A slide with images to draw on

Features used: Share a slide, Whiteboard

Description: Who doesn't like to carve a pumpkin, especially one that is not going to create a real mess? Using an image relevant to the season or the topic of the program is another fun way to warm up participants to the whiteboard tools. Often people think they cannot draw, so they resist experimenting with any of the whiteboard tools besides the text tool. This activity encourages them to try to draw using the other tools, shapes, and colors available. A simple drawing activity before the session addresses the logistics of using the whiteboard tools when there's actually time to, which allows the focus to remain on the content later, rather than struggling with the tools to perform it.

Backstory

I use this activity when I need partici-pants to be comfortable with more than the text tool. In several of the training sessions and meetings I run, we need to outline a process flow, which is best done with flowchart shapes. I also of-ten ask participants to choose a color to identify themselves during a brain-storming session on a whiteboard.

SETUP

Design needs ahead of time: Create a slide with pumpkin or other appropriate images (resize to vary them, if desired).

Before the activity begins:

Producer: Load the slide with the images. Ensure that whiteboard tools are enabled.

THE ACTIVITY

SAY	DO
Facilitator: "Welcome to our session today! As we get ready to begin our live online session today, please first use the drawing tools available on the whiteboard to have some fun and carve a pumpkin."	*Producer:* Provide guidance on the whiteboard tools as needed.
Facilitator: "Do any of these pumpkins have names? Do they have hobbies? Continue to write and draw away."	*Facilitator:* Comment on the drawings, noting anything that stands out or that you can relate to the meeting or training event.

Transition after the activity:

Facilitator: "We have enjoyed the scene you have created for us! You are all quite creative and now very skilled at using your whiteboard tools, something that will be handy later today. Let's get started on the topic of *[insert class topic here]*."

SPICE IT UP WITH THESE ALTERNATIVES

- Use any holiday image relevant to your audience: Christmas trees, menorahs, Valentine's Day hearts, Easter bunnies, snowmen, shamrocks, and so on.
- Use a partly filled-in image of a place (beach, jungle, city, mountains) and have participants complete the image.
- Use animals, flowers, or food and see what kind of fun your participants create.

Vacation Plans

Purpose: To encourage participants to get to know one another by using the whiteboard.

Session format: Meetings, Training

Audience: Any

Number of participants: Unlimited

Time: 5 to 30 minutes (before scheduled start)

Materials: A slide with images to draw on

Features used: Share a slide, Whiteboard

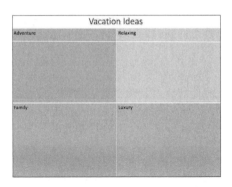

Description: As part of the welcome and audio test pre-event warm-up, use a slide like this one and have participants use the whiteboard tools to briefly write about their next vacation. Use this as an opportunity to teach them how important it is to click on the whiteboard after they finish writing so their text can be read by everyone. This activity also teaches them that pressing enter creates a line return in order to avoid going over a box or the edge of the slide. Most people do not realize a manual line return is needed in order for their entry to be seen in its entirety. Aside from introducing the tools quickly, this activity often starts conversation in the chat too, particularly when people want to go to the same places.

Backstory

Thank you to Jo Cook of the Learning & Performance Institute, a global membership body based in the United Kingdom, for sharing this simple and effective warm-up. Jo and the rest of the team can be found online at: www.learningandperformanceinstitute.com.

SETUP

Design needs ahead of time: Create a slide with four boxes providing a section for the different types of vacations people typically have (adventure, relaxing, family, and luxury).

Before the activity begins:

Facilitator: Add your own next vacation plan to set the example and share a bit about your personal life.

Producer: Load the slide. Ensure that whiteboard tools are enabled.

THE ACTIVITY

SAY	DO
Facilitator: "Welcome to our session today! Before we get started, let's make sure you know how to use the whiteboard tools. Use your text tool and share with us what your next holiday will be. Type your name next to your entry."	*Producer:* Provide guidance on the whiteboard tools as needed. *Facilitator:* Comment on the holidays, noting similarities or shared experiences.

Transition after the activity:

Facilitator: "You have all provided some wonderful ideas on holidays we could all consider for the future! Thank you! Let's get started on the topic of *[insert class topic here]*."

SPICE IT UP WITH THESE ALTERNATIVES

- Switch the topic to the participants' most recent holiday trip, their favorite holiday trip, or the one they dream about.
- Have the four boxes be about something else. For example, favorite types of restaurants (good for groups gathered online from the same area), food, movies, television shows, or books.
- Have participants describe the output of their work. The four quadrants could be "for external customers," "for internal customers," "company supporting role," and "leadership." For example, if participants work in a sales environment and select "for external customers," they might write, "I provide the right package for them," or someone in IT or HR might select "company supporting role" and then explain the specifics of their role.

Inquiring Minds Want To Know

Purpose: To engage participants at the start by asking them to think about a question for the event. Their responses will give insight into their thoughts and ideas about the upcoming meeting or training event.

Session format: Meetings, Training

Audience: Any

Number of participants: 5 to 25

Time: 15 to 30 minutes before the start of the session

Materials: A slide

Features used: Slide used as whiteboard with annotation privileges enabled, Audio, Chat, Webcam (optional)

Description: This warm-up activity can be used in so many ways for any online event by simply adjusting the question. Ask a question, wait for all participants to answer, and encourage them to discuss among themselves. Be careful

Backstory

One of the most frequent questions other facilitators ask is, "How will I know participants are paying attention and learning in my online class?" The answer is simple: ask them! Asking takes many forms, ranging from formal assessments to individual and group assignments, surveys and group discussions, formal question and answer sessions, and more. This warm-up is an effective way to find out what the participants are thinking, while getting to know the audience.

to comment appropriately with enthusiasm to foster dialogue. But most important, don't just gather the thoughts and say, "Thanks. We'll get started shortly." This does not fulfill the objective of engaging the participants from the start. If webcams are going to be used during the event, this activity is also a good time to make sure participants are seen while sharing their thoughts and comments. (But check that they are comfortable and ready before turning on the webcams.)

SETUP

Design needs ahead of time: Create a slide with the desired question (and an image of a large question mark or a face with an inquisitive look, if desired).

Before the activity begins:

Producer: Load the slide. Ensure that whiteboard tools are enabled and that public chat is available.

THE ACTIVITY

SAY	DO
Facilitator or Producer: "We will be starting in a few minutes, but as we are getting ready, we have a question for you: *[Read the question on your slide].* Please whiteboard your response."	*Producer:* Provide guidance on the whiteboard tools as needed. *Facilitator:* Respond to the participants as they answer, asking them to explain their thoughts or share more.

Transition after the activity:

Facilitator: "Thank you all so much for joining early and participating in our warm-up today. It's wonderful to get to know you as we begin our program. You shared some interesting ideas and insights, which helps me to connect the program content to your experience and background. Let's get started!"

SPICE IT UP WITH THESE ALTERNATIVES

Some sample questions to consider:

- "What comes to mind when you read, 'Customer service is our top priority'?"
- "Last week you read chapter *[Fill in number]*. What stood out for you as you think about it again now?"
- "What technical glitches have you experienced using *[Insert software name here]*? What did you do to resolve it?"
- "What are your thoughts about *[insert topic of class here]*?"

Sign In

Purpose: To add some fun to taking attendance for your event.

Session format: Meeting, Webinar, Training

Audience: Any

Number of participants: 5 to 25

Time: 15 to 30 minutes (before scheduled start)

Materials: A slide

Features used: Slide used as whiteboard with annotation privileges enabled, Chat, Audio

Welcome!
1. Guess how many and be the 1st to win a homework pass. *(Chat)*
2. Sign in by choosing your favorite flavor. *(Type your name)*

Backstory

I thought of this activity one afternoon while preparing the third class of a six-session program. I needed to take attendance each session and thought having a sign-in sheet like this would be more fun than a typical roll call or report drawn from the system. Sitting on my desk was a jar of jelly beans just like the one shown here, and I remembered a guessing game at my son's school during a holiday fair. (I never did find out how many beans were in the jar; I lost count and before I knew it they were gone.)

Description: Taking attendance is boring for everyone involved, especially participants. They wait for their name to be called and then zone out or multitask. Instead, try placing an image of a jelly bean jar on a slide and ask participants to guess the number of jelly beans in the jar. Ask them also to sign their name next to their favorite flavor. This activity stimulates the participants' minds and allows them to practice using the whiteboard tools at the same time. It also provides a colorful slide as the first thing participants see, and they can have fun chatting about favorite—or least favorite—flavors.

SETUP

Design needs ahead of time: Create a slide with the desired image and clear instructions that both indicates how attendance will be taken and how participants should answer or respond to the image.

Before the activity begins:

Producer: Load the slide. Ensure that whiteboard tools are enabled and that public chat is available.

THE ACTIVITY

SAY	DO
Facilitator or Producer: "We will be starting in a few minutes, but as we are getting ready, we thought you might like to earn a pass on your homework! Can you guess how many jelly beans are in the jar? Type your answer in the chat. And once you have done that, let us know that you are here by using the text tool to sign your name next to your favorite jelly bean flavor."	*Producer:* Provide guidance on the whiteboard tools as needed. *Facilitator:* Respond to the participants as they sign in, commenting on their guess and their favorite jelly bean. Perhaps ask them their strategy for guessing the number of jelly beans.

Transition after the activity:

Facilitator: "Thank you all so much for joining early and participating in our fun warm-up today. The correct answer is 193 jelly beans so *[Say participant name]*, you came the closest and have won *[Indicate whatever the individual won, perhaps just hearty congratulations]*. Let's get started!"

SPICE IT UP WITH THESE ALTERNATIVES

- Use an image of a world map and ask participants to enter where they have or would like to vacation.
- Use an image of a fruit salad and ask participants to choose their favorite fruit.
- Use an image of a smiley face and ask participants to collaboratively draw the rest of the person.
- Use any image related to the content or the experience of the event.

Brain Teasers

Purpose: To get participants thinking creatively while they become comfortable with the available text tools.

Session format: Meeting, Webinar, Training

Audience: Any

Number of participants: 5 to 25

Time: 15 to 30 minutes (before scheduled start)

Materials: A slide

PL**OT**	WAY _____ PASS	A CHANCE N	NOITANIMIRCSID
GONE GONE LET BE GONE GONE	GETTING IT ALL	LU CKY	PRE4SS
ME _____ IT IT IT IT IT IT IT	WORLD (circle)	chicken	WHEATHER
(vertical text)	0 MD BA PhD	LATE N E V E R	ALL / WORLD

Features used: Slides used as whiteboards with annotation privileges enabled, Audio

Description: This activity gets participants thinking critically and guessing the answers to each brain teaser. It encourages participants to learn how to use their text tools in new ways: how to change the font type, size, and color or how to move text around. An activity like this is priceless for an online event that requires annotation tools for activities later in the program.

Backstory

One weekend while cleaning out my office, I came across a box of old training materials. Among the items inside the box were activities, games, and a video from when I had participated in one of my first "train the trainer" programs many years ago. After recovering from watching the training video, I found this brain teaser on a crumpled, yellowed piece of paper. I remember enjoying the challenge of solving the teasers, and I was thankful I had scribbled all the answers on the back of the piece of paper.

SETUP

Design needs ahead of time: Create a slide with a grid pattern and the preferred brain teaser puzzles.

Before the activity begins:

Producer: Load the slide. Ensure that whiteboard tools are enabled.

THE ACTIVITY

SAY	DO
Facilitator or Producer: "We will be starting in a few minutes. As we are getting ready, we would like you to think 'inside the box.' Well, you know what we mean! Use your annotation tools and write the answers for each brain teaser directly in its box."	*Producer:* Provide guidance on the whiteboard tools as needed. *Facilitator:* Respond to the participants as they join and begin to guess the answers.

Transition after the activity:

Facilitator: "Thank you all so much for joining early and participating in our thoughtful warm-up today. Good work figuring them out. I think we are ready to stretch our minds some more and dive into the topic of *[insert event topic here]*. Let's get started!"

Note: The answers to the brain teasers included in the sample slide above are:

1. The plot thickens
2. Highway overpass
3. An outside chance
4. Reverse discrimination
5. Let bygones be bygones
6. Getting above it all
7. Lucky break
8. Foreign press
9. It's beneath me
10. As the world turns
11. Chicken little
12. A bad spell of weather
13. Get a word in edgewise
14. Three degrees below zero
15. Better late than never
16. It's a small world after all.

Mazes and Word Searches

Purpose: To have some fun with familiar activities while learning key tools in the online learning environment.

Session format: Meeting, Webinar, Training

Audience: Any

Number of participants: 5 to 25

Time: 5 to 30 minutes

Materials: A slide

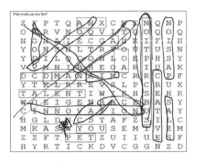

Features used: Slides used as whiteboards with annotation privileges enabled, Chat, Audio, Webcam (optional)

Description: Mazes and word searches are perfect warm-ups due to their familiarity and simplicity. Participants need little if any direction on what to do; although they may need direction on how best to use the tools to highlight, box, and change color. Use these activities when the main program involves other activities using the same tools or when participants would

benefit from thinking about the terminology used to create the puzzles. It's beneficial to encourage participants to explore the tools, rather than to just tell people where to find the answers. For instance, they can search the menu bar, or click along the annotation toolbar and explore their options, paying special attention to the dropdown arrows next to each icon. Participants often struggle with locating the toolbar, clicking on the buttons, arranging the different shapes onto the whiteboards, choosing and changing colors, choosing fonts, moving text and images, and editing or deleting text. Participants will have a better chance of learning these skills if they find these items themselves and if they explore the tools with purpose, such as navigating a maze or finding key terms in a word search.

SETUP

Design needs ahead of time: Create a slide with the desired word search, maze, or other well-known puzzle. Choosing a well-known puzzle allows the participants to have fun with something they're familiar with, while learning the tools.

Before the activity begins:

Facilitator: Use an example to demonstrate what you would like the participants to do.

Producer: Load the slide. Ensure that whiteboard tools are enabled.

THE ACTIVITY

SAY	DO
Facilitator or Producer: "We will be starting in a few minutes. In an effort to allow some practice time with the annotation tools, we've provided a *[Name the puzzle]* for your enjoyment. Use the *[Indicate the appropriate tool]* and see how you do!"	*Producer:* Provide guidance on whiteboard tools as needed. *Facilitator:* Encourage and respond to the participants as they join and begin to complete the puzzle.

Transition after the activity:

Facilitator (for a word search): "Thank you all so much for joining early and participating in our word search today. Now let's continue our discussion and work on the topics you were searching for in the puzzle."

Facilitator (for a maze): "Thank you all so much for joining early and trying to find your way through the maze. Now let's discuss some of the topics you were weaving around in the maze."

SPICE IT UP WITH THESE ALTERNATIVES

Try other common word puzzle games, such as word scrambles, cryptograms, crosswords, and so on. Visit the Discovery Education website for ideas and help with creating them: www.discoveryeducation.com/free-puzzlemaker/.

Conclusion

Trivia, vacation plans, guessing games, brain teasers, word searches, and mazes—having fun yet? These warm-up activities are just some of the many ways to engage an audience before an online event begins. Even a basic tour activity can be an engaging way to set the stage for an event, while helping participants who need preparation to use the available tools. All warm-up and welcome activities open a session with a purpose beyond telling participants to sit and listen. They set the stage for interaction and collaboration. They function as early technical checks. And they help ensure that the event starts on time and that the participants, producer, and facilitator can communicate clearly once the event starts and content-focused activities need to begin. Chapter 3 provides examples of the next activity that helps engage participants: icebreakers.

3

Let's Do This:
Breaking the Ice

. . . .

Who has time for an icebreaker in an online event? There's barely enough time to cover the critical content. So it's better to just skip the touchy-feely stuff and dive straight into the material. Right?

Wrong. Far too many online events are run as boring webinars or meetings, with dozens or hundreds in attendance (sit down), audio controls set to mute (be quiet), chat often disabled (don't interact), and the facilitator launching into lecture mode (time to multitask).

The welcome and warm-up activities in chapter 2 started the process of cracking the typical webinar and online meeting mold and making online events interactive and collaborative. This chapter introduces some effective icebreakers that can prepare participants for the main part of the online event.

Icebreakers are vital to creating an environment in which participants feel at ease enough to share opinions, ask questions, and learn something new. Because the online tools are still new for many people (even after a solid welcome or warm-up activity), participants need an additional way to connect with others who may be remotely connected and geographically dispersed. Icebreakers in an online event ensure that the participants are truly comfortable, engaged, and ready to interact. And icebreakers are especially import-ant for anyone who missed the exciting warm-up activity because they were late; they now have a second chance to learn some of the tools and get involved.

Longer introductory activities may be better suited for multisession programs than for shorter, one-session programs. The time devoted to an icebreaker depends on how much time participants will need to collaborate in the other activities. The more they need to work together, the more important the icebreaker is.

So let's see what is needed to break the online ice.

Around the World via Recipes

Purpose: To have participants share with one another and get comfortable communicating in the online environment, all through the lens of treasured recipes and friendly competition.

Session format: Meeting, Training

Audience: International, with new team members

Number of participants: 5 to 10

Time: 5 to 30 minutes (depending on how many people take a turn)

Materials: A slide for the facilitator with instructions, order of presenters, and timing; Slides for each participant; a Slide with a map of the locations and recipe or food images

Features used: Drawing tools, Audio, Chat, Presenter control (optional), Webcam (optional)

Description: This activity helps people get to know one another better, while they learn the online tools. In advance, participants are instructed to prepare a

Backstory

One Sunday afternoon, as I sat brain-storming icebreakers for a global new hire onboarding program (with my friend and colleague Paula Carr, a learning con-sultant from Herman Miller), I came up with this recipe activity. I'd recently been exploring the food in New York City since moving there earlier in the year, so food was on my mind. This activity was a per-fect blend of getting participants to open up and share with one another—and to feel comfortable communicating in the online classroom using the tools available.

slide with a picture of their favorite dish from their home country. Participants send their slides to the facilitator or producer beforehand, to be shared with the entire group once the session begins. The producer should preload all files received in advance. (If participants share their slide in the moment, it may take some time to walk them through the loading process, so prepare for that.)

Start by presenting a slide that explains the activity: participants describe their dish, what is in it, what they enjoy about it, or how it is prepared, careful not to mention the country of origin. As other participants listen, and enjoy the details, they try to guess which country it is from. The guesses are entered through the chat feature, or verbally over the audio connection as long as they do not interrupt the speaker. The speaker should be instructed to stop occasionally and look at the chat, or stop and ask if anyone has guessed it yet.

To debrief the activity, prepare a second slide with a map marking each person's location using the food image. Ask some questions to help participants connect with one another—for example, "How are we connected?" "In what ways are we linked to one another?" "What examples demonstrate that we are more than participants in an online event?"

To add a layer of competition, keep track of who guesses the most correctly and award the winner a prize.

SETUP

Design needs ahead of time: Decide if you want to create a competition by noting who guesses the most correctly. Prepare the prize.

Before the activity begins:

Producer: Load the participant slides so that participants aren't struggling with this during the activity. Ensure that public chat is available. Enable whiteboard privileges.

THE ACTIVITY

SAY	DO
Facilitator: "It's a pleasure to be connected with so many people from around the world today. Let's spend the next few moments getting to know one another through the lens of food recipes. As you know, each of you has prepared a slide with a picture of a dish that represents where you are from. We are going to take turns describing the dish, the ingredients, how it is prepared, how it is served, and maybe the historical significance as well. It's up to you. As you present, the rest of us will try to guess what country the dish and you are from. We will send our guesses using the chat. It's up to each presenter to notice and let us know when we have guessed correctly. Please finish with your description even when we have guessed. Who would like to go first? Please raise your hand."	*Producer:* Help participants load their slides if it wasn't done ahead of time.
[Participants are presenting.]	*Producer:* Ensure that the first volunteer has presenter control. Pass it to each one as they take turns. *Facilitator:* Provide encouragement and assistance to all of the presenters, including helping them notice the chat conversation and present by asking questions if they are nervous. Remind them to use their online tools: pointer, highlighter, and the like.
Facilitator: "Thank you to each person. I am really hungry now! So let's talk about what we have learned through this activity. Raise your hand to respond verbally, or feel free to respond via chat. How are we connected? What examples demonstrate that we are more than participants in an online class?"	

Transition after the activity:

Facilitator: "It is so wonderful to get to know one another and learn to use these online tools to share our experiences. Let's take a look at where we are going from here. *[Insert appropriate transitional statement for your meeting or training event.]*"

SPICE IT UP WITH THESE ALTERNATIVES

- Instead of asking participants to prepare a slide in advance, have them share a website with the recipe or a picture of the dish. To allow this, provide each attendee the proper presenter, host, or sharing controls. Guide them to then share a website. Use application sharing, desktop sharing, or web sharing. Make sure the website does not give away the recipe's country of origin unless you do not intend to have guessing as part of the activity.
- For an intact workgroup or noninternational group, use recipes that have sentimental value, and have participants share as they learn about one another. The focus could also be on the use of the live online tools of sharing slides and websites, annotating, and presenting information in an engaging way.
- Use national holidays or native holiday traditions.

Open Up

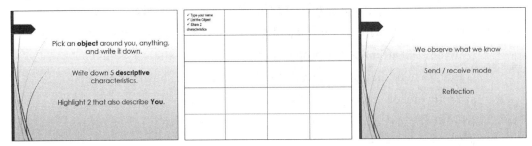

Purpose: To help trainers or other educators realize why it might be challenging for learners to accept new information, thoughts, ideas, or processes while in a learning environment; and to let participants practice with the whiteboard tool, while sharing about themselves.

Backstory

This activity is my favorite icebreaker. Some laughter, quick breathing, and sounds of shock happen every time. I once attended a "train the trainer," in-person program intended for trainers of project and time management software. Though I did not end up becoming one of those trainers, this icebreaker had such an impact on me that I rushed home and converted it for live online training. Credit goes to the person who taught the class that day. Even though I cannot remember your name, I remember your enthusiasm and I thank you for it.

Session format: Training, Meetings

Audience: Any, but works best with trainers, facilitators, and educators who need to guide an audience to learn something new

Number of participants: 5 to 25

Time: 20 minutes

Materials: Slides

Features used: Slides used as whiteboards with annotation privileges enabled, Audio, Chat, Webcam (optional)

Description: This activity works best for trainers or educators because it helps them realize why it might be challenging for learners to accept new information, thoughts, ideas, or processes while in a learning environment. It also helps trainers become better at communicating difficult or awkward information to people they may not know very well, if at all. Participants unfamiliar with one another learn about each other in unexpected ways, and intact workgroups get to experience the enjoyment of supporting one another as the details are revealed.

The activity requires just three slides. The first slide reveals the three directions, one step at a time:

1. **Pick an object.** Participants should pick an object quickly, without overthinking the selection. It's important it is an object, not another person or something intangible, like air or a feeling.

2. **Write down five characteristics.** On a piece of paper next to them, participants should write down five characteristics to describe the object, again without overthinking it.

3. **Highlight two that also describe you.** Participants should think of two of the five characteristics that describe themselves. And they should be prepared to share. On the second slide, the trainer should instruct participants to pick a box, write their name in it or use a pointer, and then write the object (or draw a picture of it) and the two characteristics.

From that moment, it becomes very interesting to watch the names, objects, and characteristics get revealed on the whiteboards. Participants are so engrossed reading each other's and waiting to hear what each person will say that it sometimes becomes very quiet. Call on two or three participants and then ask for others to volunteer if they want to explain why the two details also describe them. Try to comment on all entries even if you do not call on each person to verbally explain, as it is important to not exclude anyone.

The act of sharing information places participants in a better position to send and receive information. It is not easy to tell a group of people why you might be "shiny" or "round"; it is with thoughtful arrangement of words that you share this type of information. This icebreaker fosters a safe learning environment. While participants may not want to share these potentially awkward details made up on the spot, it is a valuable experience to hear the descriptions from others. Some will reflect on their initial reactions and realize they were driven by biases or preconceived notions about a person or a personality trait, such as when someone in the activity describes themselves as having "sharp edges" or a "green personality."

SETUP

Design needs ahead of time: Create three slides similar to those shown here. The first should have the three-step animation as described above, and the second should be used as a whiteboard.

Before the activity begins:

Producer: Ensure that public chat is available. Enable whiteboard privileges. Enable webcams (optional).

THE ACTIVITY

SAY	DO
Facilitator: "I have an icebreaker planned today that is intended just for you: trainers of those who need to learn something new. It's got a bit of a twist and requires some quick thinking and open sharing. Are you ready? Let's do it." "Choose an object around you, anything tangible, and write it down. Raise your hand when you are done."	*Producer:* Explain in the chat where the raise hand tool is located. Clear the raised hands when appropriate. Forward the slide so the next instructions appear.
Facilitator: "Now please write down five describable characteristics of this object. It is important at this time that no one shares anything and that our audio is silent, as all of us are thinking and writing down our responses. Please again raise your hand when you are done."	*Producer:* Clear the raised hands when appropriate. Forward the slide so the next instructions appear.
Facilitator: "Now highlight two of these characteristics that also describe you! Type your name, object, and the chosen two characteristics in one of the boxes on the slide. Please again raise your hand when you are done."	*Producer:* Assist participants with the whiteboard tools if necessary. Clear the raised hands when appropriate.
Facilitator: "Let's now review each of the responses. We'll start with *[Pick a participant]*—please explain your choices." [Note: If a webcam is available, allow participants to show their objects and themselves while they explain. Set the tone by sharing your object and characteristics with the participants.]	*Producer:* Highlight areas or words the trainer mentions, or as participants describe their choices.
Facilitator: "We observe what we know. Goethe said, 'We only see what we know.' The characteristics you observe most easily are also the ones with which you are most familiar. We are often drawn to what we are comfortable with, what is already known to us. This is an important point for trainers to recognize as so often participants are not comfortable learning what is new to them." **Send/Receive Mode** *Facilitator:* "This activity helped you as a trainer to facilitate more effectively by getting you into a send/receive mode. Practicing to share information that is not easy to share—for example, explaining why you are 'shiny' like the paper weight you chose—provides trainers with the opportunity to not only communicate stated ideas, but to also hear others' attempts." **Reflection** *Facilitator:* "This activity also provides us with an opportunity to share something personal and reflect on oneself. In classes where behavioral change is being requested, it is important to reflect on who we are and where we are most comfortable so we can relate better to the participants."	*Facilitator or Producer:* Build the slide as appropriate to reveal each new point.

Transition after the activity:

Facilitator: "That was certainly revealing. What will be revealed throughout the rest of today? Let's start by considering . . ."

SPICE IT UP WITH THESE ALTERNATIVES

- Use a webcam for each volunteer to allow the others to see the object and the person at the same time they describe their characteristics.
- For an intact workgroup, have them share all five characteristics and then let the others tell the group why the two also describe their teammate.

How Many Can You Name?

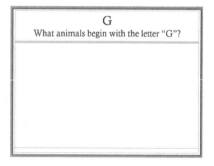

Purpose: To demonstrate the power of collective effort on a simple task, while practicing the use of the whiteboard tool at the same time.

Session format: Meeting, Webinar, Training

Audience: Any

Number of participants: Unlimited

Time: 5 to 10 minutes

Materials: A slide

Features used: Slide used as whiteboard with annotation privileges enabled, Chat, Audio

Backstory

My friend and colleague Paula Carr, a learning consultant from Herman Miller, attended an online session that led with this activity. She was surprised by its effectiveness despite its simplicity. After her experience, I knew this activity would help participants connect with one another, which they often don't in an online environment. I decided to include this activity for you to re-use and alter as much as you need! Thank you, Paula, for sharing your insight and experience.

Description: This teamwork icebreaker is a quick and simple one, and can be used with any audience for just about any topic in which working together is an outcome of the time spent together.

How many animals can you name that begin with the letter "G"? Try it. I came up with about 10. But now look at the list below—there are 100! This activity demonstrates that we can come up with so much more than we can on our own. To a large extent, our life experiences shape what we know about the world, and together we can help open one another's eyes to other possibilities.

Animals with names that begin with the letter "G":

Gadwall	Gemsbuck	Goa	Gray Squirrel
Galago	Genet	Goat	Gray Wolf
Galah	Gentoo Penguin	Godwit	Grayling
Galapagos Albatross	Gerbil	Goitered Gazelle	Great Argus
Galapagos Dove	Gerenuk	Golden Retriever	Great Dane
Galapagos Hawk	German Pinscher	Goldeneye	Great Horned Owl
Galapagos Mockingbird	German Shepherd	Golden-Mantled	Great White Shark
Galapagos Penguin	German Short-Haired	Ground Squirrel	Grebe
Galapagos Sea Lion	Pointer	Goldfinch	Greyhound Dog
Galapagos Tortoise	German Spaniel	Goldfish	Grison
Gallinule	German Spitz	Gonolek	Grizzly Bear
Galloway Cow	German Wire-Haired	Goose	Grosbeak
Gander	Pointer	Goosefish	Groundhog
Ganges Dolphin	Gharial	Gopher	Grouper
Gannet	Ghost Shrimp	Goral	Grouse
Gar	Giant Schnauzer	Gordon Setter	Grunion
Garden Snake	Gibbon	Gorilla	Guanaco
Gar-Pike	Gila Monster	Goshawk	Guernsey Cow
Garter Snake	Giraffe	Gosling	Guib
Gaur	Glassfrog	Gourami	Guillemot
Gavial	Globefish	Grackle	Guinea Fowl
Gazelle	Glow Worm	Grass Spider	Guinea Pig
Gecko	Gnat	Grasshopper	Gull
Gelada	Gnatcatcher	Gray Fox	Guppy
Gemsbok	Gnu	Gray Reef Shark	Gyrfalcon

SETUP

Design needs ahead of time: Create a simple slide with a letter clearly indicated, and the question, "What animals begin with the letter '*[letter chosen]*'?" Leave plenty of whitespace for participants to whiteboard their answers.

Before the activity begins:

Producer: Ensure that public chat is available. Enable whiteboard privileges.

THE ACTIVITY

SAY	DO
Facilitator: "How many animals can you think of that begin with the letter G? Please write them on the whiteboard."	*Producer:* Start the one-minute timer when appropriate. Assist participants with the whiteboard tools, as necessary.
Producer: "You have one minute for this activity, starting now!"	
Producer: "Your one minute is now up!" *Facilitator:* "Wow that is quite a list you've come up with together. There are common animals such as *[Name common animal]*, and some not so common ones such as *[Name uncommon animal]*. "What can we learn about working together from this experience? Please chat your thoughts."	*Facilitator:* As you and the participants discuss the results, steer them toward the realization that together the group came up with so much more than they each could have independently in the time allowed.

Transition after the activity:

Facilitator: "We collaborated so well on building that list, now let's begin the process of working on *[Insert topic of the event]*."

SPICE IT UP WITH THESE ALTERNATIVES

- Use different categories such as business terms, technical terms, and organizational terms.
- Do the entire activity using chat instead of a whiteboard if conducting a webinar.

Time Perspectives

Purpose: To share stories based on a chosen year or time period, in order to establish common ground and improve collaboration.

Session format: Meetings, Training

Audience: Any

Number of participants: 5 to 15

Time: 10 minutes

Materials: A slide

Features used: Slide used as whiteboard with annotation privileges enabled, Audio, Chat, Webcam (optional)

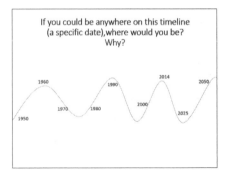

Description: This activity explores how to establish common ground among colleagues or participants in a training event. Participants answer the question, "If you could be anywhere on this timeline, where would you be and why?" They share critical life moments, key learning moments, or social events that affected their lives. They compare themes in their lives and find out where they have common topics, feelings, or experiences. Sharing these details on a timeline puts things into perspective and establishes the groundwork needed for a group of participants to open up and effectively collaborate in the event.

Backstory

What is a good icebreaker for a group of Millennials, Gen Xers, and Baby Boomers attending the same online session? After brainstorming with my colleague Sue Leo-Fitzgerald (instructional designer for Dale Carnegie Digital), we came up with Time Perspectives. By sharing stories and comparing experiences with others, relationships are enhanced through common ground. And perhaps a lasting support system will be created as a result.

If the group is an intact team, participants are more likely to open up and share deeper, more personal stories and events like marriage, divorce, and illness. If the group has not met, the topics will be lighter.

The setting of the event will also guide how people respond. It might be more focused on business topics, social events, or personal details. Participants will gravitate more to events that shaped their lives within the context of the event topic, so it is important to set the context of the event before running this activity.

SETUP

Design needs ahead of time: Create a slide that has a timeline with years appropriate to the attendees, your event's topic, and the range of stories and experiences you would like to see shared.

Before the activity begins:

Producer: Ensure that public chat is available. Enable whiteboard privileges.

THE ACTIVITY

SAY	DO
Facilitator: "I'd like to welcome each of you to the event today. Let's get to know a little more about each other, and do so from the perspective of time." "Please choose a spot on the timeline by typing your name, and then answer the question, 'If you could be anywhere on this timeline, where would you be and why?'" "Please indicate you are done using the green check [Insert alternate method as appropriate]."	*Producer:* Assist participants with the whiteboard and green check indicator, as necessary.
Facilitator: "What did you notice we have in common? What did you learn from this experience? How will you use it in today's training session? How will you use what you have learned on your team?"	*Facilitator:* Once everyone is finished, encourage participants to share their stories and examples, one at a time.

Transition after the activity:

Facilitator: "Thank you for sharing your stories, experiences, and hopes across the years. Let's see what we will be doing next in this event."

Technology Two-Step

Purpose: To help participants focus by putting away other distractions.

Session format: Meeting, Webinar, Training

Audience: Any

Number of participants: Unlimited

Time: 5 to 10 minutes

Materials: A slide

Features used: Polling, Whiteboard, Chat, Audio

Description: How do you get your online participants to turn off the other devices that distract us in today's world? Training Consultant Cindy Huggett provided a solution in the form of this activity, and said the following:

> *One of the biggest challenges we have as online trainers is to break participants'*
> *preoccupation with their work environment. Since most participants will stay at*
> *their desks to attend your virtual classes, it could be easy to address their to-do lists*
> *during the session. Even if they have good intentions to stay focused, they will be*
> *tempted by the distracting devices around them. In person, we often tell participants*
> *to put away their devices and give full attention to the class. Why not do the same*
> *online? And, better yet, why not turn it into a game?*

How it works is pretty simple. Participants identify the technology devices they have nearby, turn each device off, and then indicate that they have done so. It's a very simple approach to getting the job done, while giving participants another chance to get used to using the chat and whiteboard features of the online platform.

SETUP

Design needs ahead of time: Create a slide similar to the one here (with images of the types of technology participants likely have nearby). Create a multiple-choice/multiple-answer poll named "Technology Two-Step" that matches the images, plus add "Other" as a final response choice.

Before the activity begins:

Facilitator: Observe who is joining and help the producer greet and welcome participants.

Producer: Enable public chat. Enable the whiteboard tools.

THE ACTIVITY

SAY	DO
Facilitator: "We are about to begin our class. To prepare for the learning environment, let's play Technology Two-Step."	*Producer:* Provide guidance on the tools as needed.
Facilitator: "Which technology items do you have nearby? In the poll, please select all that apply. If you answer 'Other,' please list them on the screen (or in the chat), or draw a picture if you are so inclined. Then respond to the participants as they add items to the whiteboard."	*Producer:* Open the Technology Two-Step poll. If possible, broadcast the results while participants are responding to the question. Assist participants with instructions for how to answer the poll question, as necessary.
Facilitator: "Here comes the Technology Two-Step. Step one was identifying the technology items near you. Now, step two is to turn them into the off position, or close them down entirely."	
Facilitator: "Once you have completed step two, click the *green check* or *raise hand icon* to let us know you are ready."	*Producer:* Assist participants with instructions for using the status indicators, as necessary.

Transition after the activity:

Facilitator: "Thank you all so much for preparing your workspace for this event. Now we are ready to get started on the topic of *[Insert topic here]*."

SPICE IT UP WITH THESE ALTERNATIVES

- The facilitator names devices one by one, asking participants to "raise their hand" if they have the devices nearby. Then ask, one by one, to disable or disarm them.
- Design the activity to add some playful fun—such as award prizes for whoever has the most technology devices nearby, or whoever has the most software programs open, or whoever turns everything off and "raises her hand" first.

Three of Anything

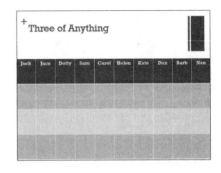

Purpose: To allow participants to learn more about each other, whether relevant to the topic of the event or not.

Session format: Meeting, Training

Audience: Any

Number of participants: 5 to 15

Time: 5 to 10 minutes

Materials: A slide

Features used: Slide used as a whiteboard with annotation privileges enabled, Audio, Chat

Description: Three of Anything is a quick icebreaker for people attending an online meeting or training event, and it can be easily adjusted to suit specific groups. Prepare a slide with a table with participants' names and spaces for items to be listed. As the session begins, ask participants to share three of their favorite places to visit, games to play, or movies to watch. Give the participants a specific time (say, one minute), and have them indicate (with a green check or raised hand) when they are finished. When appropriate, the producer calls time and clears the feedback. Encourage participants to discuss why they listed what they did, identify similarities, and share likes and even dislikes. The three items shared can truly be anything, whether it is related to getting to know one another or setting up the content of the session.

SETUP

Design needs ahead of time: Create a slide with a table, the participants' names, and space for them to whiteboard their three items.

Before the activity begins:

Producer:

- Enable public chat
- Enable the whiteboard tools
- Prepare a one-minute timer

- Prepare the breakout groups in advance and be prepared to assist the facilitator with this process (if done in breakouts).

Facilitator and producer: Indicate your responses first as examples (optional).

THE ACTIVITY

SAY	DO
Facilitator: "For this icebreaker, let's learn about what each of us like or dislike and perhaps what we share in common." "Locate your name on the board and below it, list three of your favorite *[Insert your topic here]*. We'll give you one minute, but if you are done sooner, please click on the *green check [or alternate indicator]* to let us know." *Producer:* "Your one minute starts now."	*Producer:* Provide guidance on the tools as needed. Start timer when appropriate.
Producer: "And that is one minute." *Facilitator:* "Let's take a look at what is here: what we share, where we differ, and why you listed what you did. Who would like to start? Please raise your hand." [Note: If doing this as a group breakout activity, after returning from the groups, ask for the leader of the breakout to share her lists rather than asking for a volunteer.]	*Producer:* Clear the green checks or alternate indicator used.

Transition after the activity:

Facilitator: "Thank you for that conversation starter. We clearly have a lot in common *[or not that much]*. Now we are ready to get started on *[insert class topic here]*."

SPICE IT UP WITH THESE ALTERNATIVES

- Ask participants to share three qualities of an effective leader. Ask each person to describe why and provide an example.
- For breakout groups, ask each team to select a leader who will retell the list, explaining where the group shared stories or had the same responses.

Story Time

Purpose: To get participants talking and engaged, and guard against false assumptions.

Session format: Meeting, Training

Audience: Any

Number of participants: 5 to 15

Time: 10 to 15 minutes

Materials: A slide

Features used: Share slide, Audio, Public chat, Private chat (optional)

Description: Participants bring a wealth of knowledge and experience to online sessions, so it's wrong to assume that you know all there is to know about the audience and the background they bring. In addition, participants usually love to share and hear relevant stories. It is great to get them talking before the session starts. What better way to do so than to ask them to share short stories about their experience with the session topic?

Backstory

This activity was inspired by an in-person experience at an ATD conference, where Cindy Huggett, the presenter, wanted to engage the audience before the session. The session topic was on classroom training techniques, so she asked attendees to share their most embarrassing experiences as a trainer. As the audience listened to several stories, everyone weighed in on whose story was the "best"—that is, most embarrassing. It was a lighthearted way to connect with the audience and to get the attendees involved with each other. In addition, she learned more about the audience and their experience with the session topic.

SETUP

Design needs ahead of time: Create a simple slide as a placeholder, perhaps a visual or at least wording that suggests a story activity.

Before the activity begins:

Producer: Enable public chat.

THE ACTIVITY

SAY	DO
Facilitator: "As we prepare for today's class, let's find out your experience as it relates to our topic of *[Insert class topic]*. Who is willing to tell us a brief summary of something that happened to them, related to our topic? Please raise your hand."	*Producer:* Provide guidance on the tools as needed.
	Facilitator: Respond to the participants as they share their brief stories. Encourage other participants to use their status indicators (laughter, applause) as they listen.

Transition after the activity:

Facilitator: "Thanks to each of you who shared a story. Now we are ready to get started on the topic of *[insert class topic here.]*."

SPICE IT UP WITH THESE ALTERNATIVES

Immediately pair up participants in private chat and ask them to share stories with a partner. This will increase the interaction level because participants are sharing stories in pairs, rather than listening to one story at a time in the large group. To do this, the producer can place the partners' names in the public chat. If there is an odd number, the producer or facilitator should participate.

What's Your Band Name?

Purpose: To help participants lighten up, share with others, and start to think creatively.

Session format: Meetings, Webinars, Training

Audience: Any

Number of participants: Unlimited

Time: 3 to 5 minutes

Materials: A slide

Features used: Chat

Description: Dale Carnegie said, "A person's name is to that person the sweetest most important sound in any language." We have to agree. In an online event, each person's name is clearly seen (assuming the attendee list has not been hidden and no one has logged in anonymously), so this icebreaker allows people to introduce themselves with a bit of fun attached to their real names, such as creating a fake "band" name. What better way to lighten up and learn a bit?

Backstory

I used this activity at Colin Steed's Virtual Learning Show because I was the last presenter of the conference day. I knew the attendees had introduced themselves at least three times to the other presenters before me, so I thought this would be an easy way to do introductions on my behalf, and do it with a twist at the same time. It was a big hit, kicking off the session with laughter, establishing interaction from the start, and encouraging participants to share even when it might be just a little bit embarrassing.

SETUP

Design needs ahead of time: Create a slide similar to the one shown here.

Before the activity begins:

Facilitator: Make a note of your own band name and prepare to share it.

Producer: Enable public chat.

THE ACTIVITY

SAY	DO
Facilitator: "To introduce ourselves today let's play a word game, one that perhaps allows us to learn a little more about who we 'really' might be! We will discover our band names together." "Your band name is the color of your pants and the last thing you ate. That makes mine Red Poached Eggs [Insert band name]!"	*Facilitator:* Move the slide forward to reveal the formula, share your own result, and comment as you feel is appropriate. *Producer:* Provide guidance on the chat as needed. Type your result in the chat and read some of the participants' band names out loud.
Facilitator: "So what does yours say about you? Raise your hand if you are willing to share your band name."	*Facilitator:* Comment on the band names and ask people to explain theirs.

Transition after the activity:

Facilitator: "Clearly we are all meant to be successful musicians, based on our band names alone! The topic of our event today asks us to think creatively, so let's get started on the topic of [Insert class topic here]."

SPICE IT UP WITH THESE ALTERNATIVES

- For superhero names, combine the color of your shirt and the object immediately to your right.
- For movie star names, combine your middle name and the street you grew up on.
- For *Star Wars* names, take the first three letters of your last name and add the first two letters of your first name—that's your first name. Next, take the first two letters of your mother's last name and add the first three letters of the city in which you were born—that's your last name.

Icebreaker Bingo!

Purpose: To help participants learn more about each other while at the same time become proficient using private chat.

Session format: Training

Audience: Any

Number of participants: 5 to 15

Time: 5 to 15 minutes

Materials: A slide

Features used: Public and Private Chat

Bingo!

Lead a team of more than 5 salespeople	Sold intangibles	Been in sales for greater than 10 years
Work for a global organization	Lead virtual teams	Use social media sites to network
Have had a previous Dale Carnegie training experience	Give virtual sales presentations	Have off-site sales meetings

Description: Can you play bingo in a live online training event? Of course, but it takes planning, technical knowledge, clear direction, and encouragement to make it effective online too. Participants need to know how to use the private chat, they need a board to keep their answers on, and then they need to be kept on track with time. It's important to keep checking in with them, usually over the audio, so you don't let anyone get lost by not participating. Since you cannot see them privately chatting, verbal assistance will make the difference.

Backstory

I always thought bingo was a pretty fun and energetic way to get to know other participants in face-to-face training sessions, so I really wanted to make it work online too. Thank you to Abbe Hersing, senior instructional designer at Dale Carnegie Training, for the sample bingo card from one of the sales training courses she designed.

SETUP

Design needs ahead of time: Create a slide with nine boxes, each with a fact, a place, or an experience connected to the attendees of the session.

Before the activity begins:

Facilitator: Prepare a bingo card similar to the one above, but related to your attendees, so the choices on the card will actually apply to them.

Producer: Be ready to assist participants with the private chat. Be ready to keep track of timing and verbally announce it.

THE ACTIVITY

SAY	DO
Facilitator: "Welcome to our session today! Let's spend some time going around the virtual room getting to know one another. You see nine boxes on the table, each containing a simple fact or other bit of information. Using private chat, send messages to find out more about one another and who can claim any of these as their own. As soon as you learn something that is in one of the boxes, whiteboard your initials in the box on the slide. I will also be participating along with you. The first one to get us to three across, diagonal, or vertical wins the game!" "Raise your hand and be prepared to prove your answers by telling who meets the criteria in each of the boxes you marked. Take three minutes."	*Facilitator*: Participate in the game too. *Producer*: Help attendees use the private chat and whiteboard tools as needed. Announce when there is one minute remaining and when time has run out.
Facilitator: "It looks like we have a winner! Let's hear from [Say winner's name] to learn more about what [he/she] discovered."	*Facilitator*: Encourage the sharing of details and for those who answered yes to any of the facts to tell their stories. Encourage others who did not win to share what they learned too. Debrief based on the time you have allotted for the entire activity.

Transition after the activity:

Facilitator: "You've worked hard to learn more about one another and to share about yourselves. Let's get started on the topic of [insert class topic here]."

SPICE IT UP WITH THESE ALTERNATIVES

- See who can complete the entire board first, rather than completing a row. This takes longer so only use this version if you have time to spare.
- Place participants in teams of two or three, using breakouts.
- Allow participants to move from breakout to breakout learning about one another using the audio instead of just the chat. (Note that the online platform must allow participants to move themselves around breakouts in order for this to work.)

First-Name Acronym

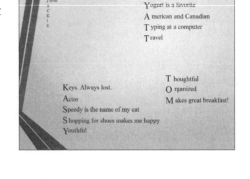

Purpose: To help participants learn more about each other while they share more about themselves.

Session format: Training

Audience: Any

Number of participants: 5 to 15

Time: 5 to 15 minutes

Materials: A slide

Features used: Share Slide, Whiteboard

Description: Remembering a person's name is not easy to do. It requires focus, determination, and practice. Online we have an attendee list to view so remembering a person's name can be easy. But remembering details about who shared what story or who had which question is not.

Encouraging people to share more about themselves than just their names and job titles will help everyone get to know each other. This will transform the online event and help participants make authentic connections. This activity takes just a few minutes yet it can be very powerful. Simply have participants write their names vertically on a whiteboard. Adjacent to each letter along the right side, have them write a word that begins with that letter that describes them. Participants then take turns introducing themselves, using the words they have shared on the whiteboard.

Backstory

Thank you to Abbe Hersing, senior instructional designer at Dale Carnegie Training, for this activity, and Jackie Regan, trainer at Dale Carnegie, for the alternatives provided below.

SETUP

Before the activity begins:

Facilitator: Think of your own and be prepared to add yours as an example.

THE ACTIVITY

SAY	DO
Facilitator: "Welcome to our session today! Let's all write our first names vertically on a whiteboard. Adjacent to each letter along the right side, write a word that begins with that letter that describes you. You have *[Announce how many minutes allotted for activity]* minutes to do this. Then get ready to introduce yourself to each other using these words!"	*Producer:* Help attendees use the whiteboard tools as needed. Keep track of time.
[Participants introduce themselves by going over the words they chose.]	*Facilitator and Producer:* Comment on every participant's introduction as appropriate.

Transition after the activity:

Facilitator: "It's been a pleasure getting to know each of you! Let's get started on the topic of *[insert class topic here]*."

SPICE IT UP WITH THESE ALTERNATIVES

Use a word that fits the topic of the online event, such as "SPEAK" for presentation training, "CULTURE" for diversity training, "VIRTUAL" for live online trainer training, "PRODUCE" for live online producer training, "BRIDE" for an online bridal shower, and "CHRISTINE" if Christine is retiring.

Conclusion

Moving beyond warm-up and welcome activities, icebreakers are vital to creating an environment in which participants feel at ease enough to share opinions, ask questions, and learn something new. Participants benefit from additional, fun ways to engage with others who may be remotely connected and geographically dispersed. Icebreakers in an online event ensure that the participants are truly comfortable, engaged, and ready to interact. And they are especially important for anyone who missed the exciting warm-up activity because they were late; they now have a second chance to learn some of the tools and get involved.

The next three chapters provide activities meant for the main part of an online event, separated out by event type: meetings, webinars, and training programs.

4

Get Active:
Engaging Virtual Meetings

· ·

Online meetings are not always easy to run—or attend. They are usually delayed due to technical problems such as using the incorrect login information, whether invitations were sent and received, audio confusion, and, of course, failing to preload slides and resorting to the share desktop feature instead.

What is the role of the producer in online meetings, and is it a necessity to have one? In short, a producer is optional for an online meeting. Some meetings will benefit from them, while others don't require them. Meeting facilitators will likely know if they need one, because they may not know how to log in, start the meeting, or invite the participants, let alone feel completely comfortable with the technology involved in the planned activities.

There are also many technical details that can affect the effectiveness of the virtual meeting:

- Will it be over the phone, or using audio through a computer, or both?
- Will participants use headsets to optimize their audio?
- Does the meeting have a link, and do participants have it?
- Can international members join the meeting?
- Will the slides look as designed, and will the transitions work well if there are multiple presenters?

Knowing the platform and its capabilities is essential. Presenters and meeting leaders need to step up and learn the technology. They also need to say to attendees, "Here's what's expected." Meetings are not just about the content. For participants, they are about much more than clicking a link and showing up.

Consequently, interaction is critical. Virtual meeting presenters need to continually monitor the chat and respond to questions and comments as quickly as possible. An effective way to give feedback in a virtual meeting, chat can also be a place where meeting participants' voices are heard (seen). It shouldn't feel distracting if people use chat—in fact, it is distracting if they don't. Encourage everyone to use chat to ask questions, make comments, and add ideas, which makes the meeting seem like a normal flow of dialogue. Effective virtual team meeting leaders watch what is going on there, only limiting the conversation if participants say things that are far off topic or significantly inappropriate.

Backstory

Therese Owen, senior product manager at Dale Carnegie Digital, said, "When I first encountered chat in a meeting, my conventional sensibilities kicked in: Why are people chatting when this important person is talking? Over time I began to realize the chat was like that nod in the meeting, or the glance you get, or that quick comment you can relate to that often gets missed in a virtual meeting. People can build off each other and then the meeting presenter knows they are paying attention."

Great Virtual Teams

Working on a virtual team can be a wonderful experience if it is inclusive, personal, and productive. It requires active and purposeful communication and team building that breaks the traditional mold of going into the office every day and taking a seat at a desk in a cubicle or office. Well-designed and well-executed virtual meetings are a crucial aspect of strong virtual teams.

However, it should be noted that on their own, virtual meetings are not enough. What makes a great virtual team work is knowing when each person is available and communicating with others. Here are some regular tasks that make a virtual team work well together:

- Establish a standard instant messaging program for the team and require participation as follows:
    - Remain logged-on during work hours.
    - Maintain appropriate status notifications such as Away, Available, Do Not Disturb, and so on.
    - For extended time away, post a status update such as "Tuesday: available between 8 a.m. and 3 p.m. EST only."
- Announce new team members through email (and instant messaging).
- Recognize personal accomplishments, professional milestones, and work anniversaries through email (and instant messaging).
- If available, use an intranet social media site (with discussion forums, status updates, and blogs) to encourage collaboration, idea-sharing, and more.
- If possible, meet in person once a year or as often as needed for traditional team building and relationship development.

When the Society for Human Resource Management studied virtual teams, it found that, "approximately half (51 percent) of HR professionals who say their companies use virtual teams said that building team relations is an obstacle that prevents them from being successful" (Minton-Eversole 2012). While great virtual meetings alone won't be enough to resolve this obstacle and make a virtual team successful, they are a necessary component. What helps to make virtual meetings interactive and engaging are great activities—ones that turn passive attendees into active participants. This chapter provides the virtual meeting activities to do just that.

Recognize and Celebrate

Purpose: To honor the accomplishments of members of a team or an organization.

Session Format: Meeting

Audience: Any

Number of participants: Unlimited

Time: 2 to 5 minutes

Materials: A slide

Features used: Share a slide, Webcam

Description: When running an online meeting, it's easy to skip over some of the traditional agenda items that are covered during in-person meetings, like taking a moment to recognize the accomplishments of the meeting attendees. It's common to jump right into the meeting agenda, to perhaps make up for the lost time from starting late. But taking the time to create a slide to celebrate the accomplishments of team members or special guests at the meeting—a little recognition—goes a long way in creating and supporting a committed virtual team as well as a more positive meeting atmosphere. It doesn't require much effort or time but can make a huge impact. Examples of accomplishments to celebrate include work anniversaries; milestones or goals met; birthdays; get well wishes; or even more personal events, such as weddings and birth announcements.

SETUP

Design needs ahead of time: Create a slide that contains a picture of the person and the accomplishment or the other relevant information shown in a celebratory way—be creative.

Before the activity begins:

Facilitator: Confirm that the information regarding the recognition or celebration is in fact accurate and still applicable. Learn the details to appropriately announce it in the meeting.

Producer: Load the slide. Enable webcams. Provide assistance as needed.

THE ACTIVITY

SAY	DO
Facilitator: "As we begin our meeting today, I'd like to take a moment to recognize *[name]* for *[description of anniversary, milestone, or other event]*! Congratulations!	*Facilitator:* Share appropriate details, or a story if possible, and then allow the person to say a few words as appropriate. *Producer:* Assist those on webcams as necessary.

Transition after the activity:

Facilitator: "What a pleasure it is to get to not only work with each of you but to celebrate with you too! Let's review our agenda for today's meeting."

SPICE IT UP WITH THIS ALTERNATIVE

Order a gift online and have it shipped directly to the person. Grab a screenshot of the gift and place it on a second slide. Recognition that takes the additional step to appear in person in an online world will make a lasting impression, one that is sure to be talked about during the years to come.

The Collaborative Agenda

Purpose: To get everyone involved in the meeting immediately and to give everyone a chance to be heard.

Session Format: Meeting

Audience: Any

Number of participants: Unlimited

Time: 5 minutes

Materials: A slide, left blank

Features used: Share slide, Whiteboard

Description: Creating and distributing an agenda are common best practices when planning and running an effective meeting, both in-person and online. A major obstacle to overcome when conducting an online meeting is convincing meeting attendees to become active participants. To engage the attendees, try kicking off a meeting with active participation by asking presenters to collaborate on the agenda. This entails writing the planned agenda on the board as people join the meeting, not just creating the topics on the fly. Meeting presenters should be aware that they will be providing an update and speaking so they won't be surprised or sense that the meeting has no direction. If appropriate, ask meeting attendees to whiteboard their ideas for additional agenda items if time allows.

During the meeting, the agenda can be revisited and meeting attendees can take notes on it, add checkmarks as tasks are completed, and add new topics that come up. The meeting agenda becomes a live collaboration and in some cases a record to be saved and distributed once the meeting is over.

SETUP

Design needs ahead of time: Make an agenda slide that is part of the meeting presentation, but leave it blank, rather than filling it in ahead of time.

Before the activity begins:

Facilitator: Confirm each meeting presenter will be attending the meeting. Inform meeting presenters that they will be providing their update or input at a designated time and will be requested to add it to the agenda slide.

Producer: Load the presentation. Ensure that the agenda slide is ready. Enable the whiteboard tools. Provide whiteboard tool assistance if needed.

THE ACTIVITY

SAY	DO
Facilitator: "Welcome *[meeting presenter]*! As you join our meeting today, add your agenda item on the whiteboard."	*Facilitator:* Encourage attendees to use the whiteboard tools as soon as they join. *Producer:* Provide help as needed.
Facilitator: "What else should we add to the agenda today? Let's take notes on this same whiteboard, and as we complete each item, check them off the list. Thanks!"	*Facilitator:* Revisit the agenda as needed, but allow time for other presentations to be loaded, or other presenters to screen share as needed.

Transition after the activity:

Facilitator: "Continue to take notes. This agenda is a place for all meeting participants to contribute and actively keep track of the meeting together. We can revisit it as needed. For now, *[first presenter]* it's time for your update."

SPICE IT UP WITH THIS ALTERNATIVE

Place each meeting contributor's name on the agenda slide and have him type next to his name. This provides some structure rather than a completely blank agenda slide.

What Can We Learn?

Purpose: To debrief the lessons learned from a project.

Session Format: Meeting

Audience: Any

Number of participants: Unlimited

Time: 15 to 30 minutes

Materials: A slide, left blank

Features used: Share slide, Whiteboard

Description: The virtual meeting is the perfect place to gather team members together at the completion of a project to discuss the lessons learned. A simple example is to enable the whiteboard tools for all participants and ask them to share their ideas. Using a simple brainstorming approach, each person types on the slide, arranges the ideas into categories (positives, negatives, room for improvement), discusses as necessary, and then documents the actionable items to implement any process changes for future projects. Save the whiteboard results and distribute any necessary information to the team members for action items they may be responsible for in the future.

SETUP

Design needs ahead of time: Make a What Can We Learn? slide, left mostly blank to allow for whiteboarding space.

Before the activity begins:

Facilitator: When inviting team members to the meeting, let them know the purpose of the meeting (or this part of the meeting) in advance to ensure that they are prepared to debrief the lessons learned.

Producer: Ensure that the slide is ready. Enable the whiteboard tools. Provide whiteboard tool assistance if needed.

THE ACTIVITY

SAY	DO
Facilitator: "This project has been very successful for us as a team and as an organization. We have exceeded the client's expectations and learned new ways to operate efficiently in the process. Let's brainstorm what we have learned to add these lessons to an improved process for future projects. Please use the whiteboard tools to share your thoughts."	*Producer:* Provide help with the whiteboard tools as needed.
	Facilitator: Continue the meeting this way, encouraging discussion and clarification as it progresses. *Producer:* Save the whiteboards and assist with distribution after the meeting as needed.

Transition after the activity:

Facilitator: "This has been an excellent meeting *[or activity]*, providing us with the lessons learned from an important project in order to improve our processes moving forward. Thank you all for your thoughtful contributions. Let's review the action items we came up with."

SPICE IT UP WITH THESE ALTERNATIVES

- Call it "Little-Known Facts" and run it as a meeting icebreaker to get to know team members. Have participants write a little-known fact about themselves on the whiteboard, without signing their name to it. Participants guess which person wrote what. Debrief by making one of the following points: we shouldn't judge a book by its cover; sometimes we have things in common with people we never thought we would; or how this was a great way to get to know people.
- Call it "Where Are We Starting?" and use this activity to set a baseline knowledge level at the beginning of a project. Align team members on what is being created or accomplished, and establish milestone project steps that everyone understands.
- Call it "Midway Check Point" and use this activity to learn project and milestone progress. Encourage discussion to identify gaps and action items to get realigned or back on track. Have team members write details about the project from their perspectives to create open communication.

Person of the Day

Purpose: To celebrate or otherwise focus on one random person for the particular meeting.

Session Format: Meeting

Audience: Any

Number of participants: Unlimited

Time: 2 to 5 minutes

Materials: A slide

Features used: Share a slide, Webcam

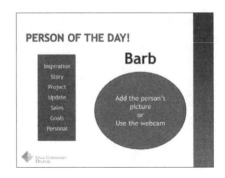

Description: Say there are 10 to 15 people on a team, all of whom would really benefit if the members learned more about each other. Rather than trying to fit this into one meeting, use this activity to spread out the learning by highlighting one or two at a time over a few weeks. The "Person of the Day" activity allows people to contribute to the online meeting and talk about themselves in a way that is planned, easy, and comfortable.

This activity fits best with regularly scheduled team meetings. In advance of the meeting, select a theme to focus on for several weeks. It could be a moment of inspiration or a lesson learned. It could be a personal story, a successful project, a fascinating news article, an important sale closed, or perhaps a team member achieved a personal or professional goal. It could also be a personal story or fact that the team doesn't know. Before the meeting, let the people on the team who are scheduled to present know that they will be presenting. Start the meeting by giving these people one to two minutes to tell their story.

SETUP

Design needs ahead of time: Select a theme to focus on for several weeks. Inform the person that he has been chosen to participate in this activity for the meeting. Prepare the slide with the person's photo. Have a timer ready to keep the person on track with his story.

Before the activity begins:

Facilitator: Remind the "Person of the Day" that it is his turn, so that he isn't surprised or upset that he was asked to open the meeting. Ask the "Person of the Day" to limit the story to two minutes.

Producer: Load the slide. Enable webcams. Provide assistance as needed, including tracking the time.

THE ACTIVITY

SAY	DO
Facilitator: "Our theme for this week is 'inspiration' and *[speaker name]*, you're up. Please share with the group."	*Facilitator:* Encourage the speaker to continue if the speaker falters in telling the story or is nervous being on the webcam. Remind the group that everyone will be doing this in future meetings. *Producer:* If necessary, give the speaker a 15-second warning when he needs to wrap up so that you keep the meeting on track.

Transition after the activity:

Facilitator: "Thank you, *[name]* and congratulations! We look forward to hearing from *[name]* next week. Let's continue now with the rest of our meeting."

SPICE IT UP WITH THESE ALTERNATIVES

- Ask the speaker to tell a story from the past week.
- Ask the speaker to talk about an exciting or interesting current project.
- Ask the speaker to provide an update on a key client.
- Ask the speaker to mention any goals met or working on.
- Ask the speaker to describe something personal like an event or a vacation.

Pros and Cons

Purpose: To brainstorm the pros and cons of a decision or other similar topic.

Session Format: Meeting

Audience: Any

Number of participants: Unlimited

Time: 10 minutes

Materials: A slide or note

Features used: Chat, Note pod or a slide, Audio

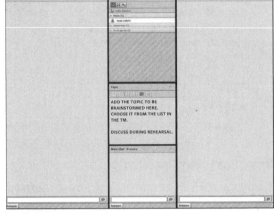

Description: Brainstorming is a common way to gather data, information, opinions, or evidence in business situations. During in-person meetings, brainstorming can be very effective, but it can easily be derailed when one person takes over or after the first few ideas are shared. In some sense, the virtual environment supports the true nature of brainstorming. There are no judgments or opinions, and one person can't as easily dominate the conversation. Since participants are usually logging in by themselves, there is more time to focus and think about the brainstorm, and the physical distractions from the other meeting participants are simply not present.

In "Pros and Cons," use separate chat pods for the pros and cons of an issue, and place a note pod in the center to remind people of the topic being brainstormed. Provide a time limit to keep the meeting and the brainstorm itself on track. Use a countdown timer and announce it over the audio. The timer found at http://e.ggtimer.com is one option that is easy to use.

SETUP

Design needs ahead of time: Create a note pod or a slide with the topic to be brainstormed. Decide how much time you want to give meeting participants to brainstorm.

Before the activity begins:

Facilitator: Clarify how the brainstorm will work: using chat, one topic at a time, timed, discussion to follow, and so on.

Producer: Ensure that directions are loaded (note pod or a slide). Enable public chat. Provide assistance as needed, including tracking the time.

THE ACTIVITY

SAY	DO
Facilitator: "For today's meeting, let's take some time to brainstorm the pros and cons of launching a new project to *[Update our website, etc.].* You'll see an area on the left to brainstorm the 'pros' and one on the right for the 'cons.' We are going to do them one at a time, for exactly one minute each. Let's start with the pros. Think of as many as you can and just type them as they come."	*Producer:* Keep track of time and announce when one minute is up.
Facilitator: "Now that we've spent a minute on the pros, take another minute to review the list and determine if you would like to add more to it."	*Producer:* Keep track of time and announce when one minute is up.
Facilitator: "Now let's repeat this process for the cons. You will have one minute here as well."	*Producer:* Keep track of time and announce when one minute is up.

Transition after the activity:

Facilitator: "We have gathered so many ideas in such a short amount of time. Let's now begin to sift through them, clarifying and understanding each so we categorize them and decide upon next steps and action items."

SPICE IT UP WITH THESE ALTERNATIVES

- If you are not using Adobe Connect, simply use the main chat area twice. Type "PROS" in the chat and keep time. Add a chat delineator like "**********" and then type "CONS" and keep time. This will help identify the brainstorm when you save the chat for viewing later.
- Try using a whiteboard instead. Use a T-Chart with the pros on the left and cons on the right. Perform the brainstorm in the spaces provided on the whiteboard.
- Break the participants into smaller groups to focus on different components, or hold a broader discussion at another meeting to explore the best solution.
- Create a poll and have participants vote on brainstormed ideas, selecting their top one or two choices.
- Have participants offer their ideas on audio while one person gathers notes on a whiteboard.

Prioritize

Purpose: To prioritize a topic.

Session Format: Meeting

Audience: Any, but might be most appropriate for a group of managers or a leadership team

Number of participants: Unlimited

Time: 30 minutes

Materials: A slide with areas to whiteboard

Features used: Whiteboard, Audio

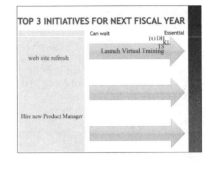

Description: Most departments, committees, and teams will face more options or project possibilities than they can accomplish during the time allowed. So prioritizing what is really important becomes critical. This can be done in a virtual meeting just as well as an in-person meeting, perhaps even more effectively. Prioritizing in a virtual meeting may even reduce the chances that a single person will dominate the discussion.

For this activity, you need to already have a list of items to prioritize. If you don't, start with a whiteboard area to brainstorm the items. Once a list is ready, each item needs to be prioritized. This can be done democratically with everyone in the group indicating where the item falls on a 1 to 10 scale, or a "Can Wait" to "Essential" scale. Vary how the votes are shown depending on the situation—for example, by initials or by generic indicators if there are confidentiality concerns.

The facilitator should be ready if the votes do not demonstrate a consensus of which items are highest priority. If this occurs, some discussion will need to ensue about what the group's goals are.

SETUP

Design needs ahead of time: Create a slide with space to type and arrows to indicate priority levels.

Before the activity begins:

Producer: Ensure that the slide or whiteboard is loaded. Enable the annotation and whiteboard tools.

THE ACTIVITY

SAY	DO
Facilitator: "We need to determine the top three initiatives we should focus on for the next fiscal year. Using your text tool, click somewhere on the purple box, then type your name, then type the top initiative you think your group should be working on. What is it from your perspective? Once you've clicked and typed your response, click off of it so we can all see what you've typed."	*Producer:* Manage the whiteboard as needed. Explain where to find the text tool if necessary.
Facilitator: "Thank you, this is a good list. Let's now take each of these ideas, and indicate the priority level we think it deserves. Please use your initials [or generic symbol] to mark the priority of each."	*Facilitator:* After they have done this, move one of the initiatives from the left box to the arrow on the right and have each person place a star or checkmark according to his or her opinion of the importance of the item for the coming year.
Facilitator: [Lead a discussion of each initiative, noting the consensus priority levels, etc.]	*Producer:* Rearrange the initiatives listed in the purple box over to the beginning of the top arrow.

Transition after the activity:

Facilitator: "Now that we have a better view of our beliefs on what is important, let's take the top three and begin to work through our next steps and action items."

Meet Your Goals

Purpose: To collaborate to create ideas and actions for reaching revenue or other goals for a group.

Session Format: Meeting

Audience: Any, but especially for a group of managers or a leadership team

Number of participants: 5 to 8

Time: 15 to 60 minutes

Materials: Whiteboards

Features used: Whiteboard, Audio

GOALS - let's brainstorm how we get to the finish line

Goal 1
idea
idea
idea
idea
Goal 2
idea
idea
idea
Goal 3
idea
idea
idea
idea
Goal 4
idea
idea
idea

Description: This activity involves members of the group typing ideas onto a slide with a whiteboard, in order to reach the group's goals. Following this initial brainstorm, the group discusses each idea, asks clarifying questions, and ensures that everyone understands the relative merits of each. The next step is to vote on the top three each member thinks are the most realistic and likely to help in reaching the goal or goals. The top vote-getters (say, the top five) are copied onto a new whiteboard, and a leader is assigned for each, along with initial action items to begin work on immediately. Finally, the group decides when and how often they will meet to report on progress.

Backstory

One of the most efficient online meetings I've been part of was when my team and I gathered to collaborate on ways we could increase revenue as we neared the end of a fiscal year. It was done in a standing weekly online meeting using just a whiteboard, the annotation tools, and audio for a lively discussion. It would no doubt work just as well for any similar goals-related brainstorm session.

SETUP

Design needs ahead of time: Prepare a whiteboard (or several) on which group members can write.

Before the activity begins:

Facilitator: Inform attendees of the intent of the meeting ahead of time so they come prepared with ideas.

Producer: Enable the whiteboard tools.

THE ACTIVITY

SAY	DO
Facilitator: "We have a real opportunity to make a difference this year. As we come to the third quarter close, let's put our minds together to find out what we can do to increase revenue as we head into the fourth quarter. Type your ideas on the whiteboard."	*Producer:* Assist with the whiteboard tools, as necessary. *Facilitator:* Discuss and clarify the ideas as they are added, as necessary.
Facilitator: "Now take a moment to review these so we can each vote on the top three ideas we think are realistically achievable and the most impactful. Any questions? If not, then please place a star next to your choices."	
Facilitator: "Now that we can see which ones have the most votes, let's narrow the list, determine a leader for each, and identify the first action items."	*Producer:* Add another whiteboard and copy and paste the top three or five items the team wants to work on. *Facilitator:* Record the decisions regarding leaders and action items for each idea.

Transition after the activity:

Facilitator: "Excellent work team! Let's regroup at the same time next week, for a check on our progress."

Mime It

Purpose: To provide a chance for team building during an online meeting.

Session Format: Meeting

Audience: Any

Number of participants: Unlimited

Time: 5 to 15 minutes

Materials: An ordered list of meeting attendees

Features used: Webcam, Note pod or a slide with the ordered list of attendees, Audio

Description: Being a member of a virtual team is challenging—but also rewarding. You can often be more productive and more focused, and have greater flexibility, job satisfaction, and work-life balance. But working with people whom you might not know as well as you might if you worked in an office together can make collaboration difficult. Global time zones, cultural differences, and a lack of technology add to the reasons why virtual teams may have trouble functioning.

Backstory

I used to think webcams were a feature of an online meeting useful only for introducing oneself and then turning off to get to the real purpose of the meeting. However, the longer I have worked on a virtual team, the more webcam willing I have become! One of the best ways I have seen a group of people build "team relations" was by using the webcam all at the same time in a virtual meeting to play Mime It. The laughter could be heard throughout the Internet, I'm certain!

This activity takes virtual teams to new interaction levels by requiring everyone to be on the webcam at the same time while each person takes a turn pantomiming an action and then passing it the next team member. So, for example, you might act like you are reading a book, and then make a point to pass that book to a fellow team member, who then reads the book too, indicating she understands your mime and that you successfully communicated your action. That colleague then might act like she is casting a fishing line and reeling in a big fish. She would then hand the pole to the next team member who tries to unhook the fish. Each person takes a turn responding to an action, and then creating a new one to pass to the next team member until each person has taken a turn. Make sure to post a list of attendees so that the order is clear. Also, keep the chat open so team members can help each other guess if the mime is not as clear.

SETUP

Design needs ahead of time: Prepare a note pod or a slide with the entire list of attendees to establish the order of pantomimes.

Before the activity begins:

Facilitator: Establish the order of pantomimes. Explain who each person is to mime to next. Ask each group member to be webcam-ready.

Producer: Ensure a list of attendee order is visible. Enable webcam rights.

THE ACTIVITY

SAY	DO
Facilitator: "In today's meeting, let's put our teamwork and communication skills to the test. Each of us will take a turn pantomiming an action while on the webcam. Be sure to make it very clear, because your colleague needs to mime the action. Tom, you begin and pass it to Kassy. From there, Kassy, it's your turn to create an action to pass to Therese. Ready everyone? Go!"	*Facilitator:* Help people recall whom they are passing to and then when it is the next person's turn, if necessary. *Producer:* Encourage other team members to use chat to help guess the actions when people need it.
Facilitator: "Now that we have gone around and each of you has taken a turn, who can tell me why we did this? Raise your hand!"	*Facilitator:* Respond to their comments and ideas, ensuring the following points are made: Clear communication is critical to team success. Our actions are sometimes misunderstood and clarification or assistance is required to proceed. Taking a risk to step out of one's comfort zone can help us get to know one another better, and allow us to have a little fun doing it.

Transition after the activity:

Facilitator: "That was fun! Clear communication is key to our team's overall success, and getting to know one another is key to better communication! Way to go on this activity!"

SPICE IT UP WITH THESE ALTERNATIVES

- If there is less time, have the group play virtual "hot potato" instead.
- Have group members act out a short scene, one after another.
- Have group members display the same emotion or expression on webcam at the same time (angry, sad, excited, happy).

Conclusion

Virtual meetings are not always easy to run or attend. The best ones have facilitators that continuously monitor the chat and respond to questions and comments as quickly as possible. In many cases, activities can be what turn a mediocre virtual meeting into an outstanding one that informs and motivates participants to action while providing a relaxed and fun experience.

The next chapter provides activities that are geared toward online events with potentially very large audiences: webinars.

Reference

Minton-Eversole, T. 2012. "Virtual Teams Used Most by Global Organizations, Survey Says." Organizational and Employee Development Blog, July 19. Alexandria, VA: Society of Human Resource Management. www.shrm.org/hrdisciplines/orgempdev /articles/pages/virtualteamsusedmostbyglobalorganizations,surveysays.aspx# sthash.20SSL96x.dpuf.

5

Perform on the Virtual Stage: Engaging Webinars

· ·

As the Introduction noted, this book uses "webinar" to refer to a live online presentation for an audience ranging from tens to hundreds or even thousands of attendees. Webinars pose unique challenges for facilitators to take the stage and engage their large online audiences. It takes special focus and attention to storytelling, the pitch and tone of voice, and the strengths of the technology platform to avoid delivering boring lectures. Well-designed webinars also include activities that cater to the size of the audience, and this chapter provides some examples.

For webinars with large audiences comprising mostly strangers, dealing with silence is a primary challenge. This is when attempts to engage an audience are met with no response—not in the chat and not over audio. It's so quiet everyone can hear the crickets chirping outside everyone else's window.

Industry expert Roger Courville notes that while there can be silence during in-person presentations, online audiences almost expect to be passive participants in virtual presentations and classes—to be talked at, rather than to be engaged in a dialogue. To combat this, he uses an "On the Way in the Door" opening activity, similar to the "Inquiring Minds Want to Know" activity in chapter 2. In his version, he starts by wondering aloud why attendees aren't greeted by the facilitator as they arrive, like they do for in-person seminars. He asks that while the virtual attendees get settled, they share something interesting with him and the group. For example, "Where are you joining from today?" or "How many cups of coffee have you had this morning?" or "What's the craziest thing you've ever done?"

Starting your webinar with this kind of welcome activity helps engage the audience. And it may even help eliminate any silence that might occur during the event because it gets the audience talking from the very beginning. The activities that follow are designed to maintain the engagement momentum throughout the webinar event.

Finish This Sentence

Purpose: To engage a webinar audience to think about the topic and share their opinions.

Session format: Webinar

Audience: Any

Number of participants: 100+

Time: 5 minutes

Materials: A slide

Features used: Share presentation, Chat

Description: An easy way to engage a webinar

audience is to simply ask a question—and instead of using a poll, let the attendees respond in their own words using chat. This activity could be used at any time during a webinar, including as an opener. While the idea of reading all the responses may seem daunting, remember that the point of the activity is not necessarily to read every single response. The point is to create interaction with the participants. The feedback may even offer some guidance on how to proceed through the presentation. Read as many as possible, confirm that the participants are present and paying attention, and respond out loud to anticipated responses. This dialogue creates an energy that will endure through the webinar.

SETUP

Design needs ahead of time: Create a PowerPoint file with the opening of a sentence relevant to the topic—for example, "An engaging webinar will . . ."

Before the activity begins:

Facilitator: Review the question and think of possible answers. Prepare a response to the answers to use as talking points throughout the presentation.

Producer: Ensure the chat is enabled and viewable by all participants.

THE ACTIVITY

SAY	DO
Facilitator: "As we begin to identify the techniques you can use to engage a webinar audience, let's open this segment of the presentation by completing the following sentence. Using chat, finish this sentence: 'An engaging webinar will . . .'."	*Producer:* If the facilitator needs help reading the chats, prepare to read some of the responses out loud. *Facilitator:* Respond to some of the answers as they come through like it is a conversation—or a "chatversation."
Facilitator: "'Be clear and move quickly,' 'include storytelling,' 'give me tips I can use immediately,' 'have no technical issues,' 'provide resources to use after the webinar.' Yes! These are all great answers. Let's look at ways we can do these things every time we present a webinar."	

Transition after the activity:

Facilitator: "Many of you mentioned that an engaging webinar will . . . 'have no technical issues.' Let's look next at three things you can do to manage and minimize any technical problems that may occur."

How Things Change

Purpose: To identify different generations of people attending your webinar.

Session format: Webinar

Audience: Any

Number of participants: 100+

Time: 5 minutes

Materials: A slide

Features used: Share presentation, Chat

Description: The How Things Change activity can be used as a tool to find out some details about who is participating in the webinar. Because most participants do not use the webcam while in a webinar, it can be difficult to know how to tailor the talk and what examples would resonate the most. A registration list will include industry, specific company, and role of participants, but it might not reveal their generation. So during the chat ask participants to list an example of a technology that did not exist when they were 10 years old.

Backstory

Thanks to Nanette Miner, the Training Doctor (www.trainingdr.com), for contributing How Things Change. She usually runs this as an activity in a training event, using a whiteboard or sometimes breakout groups. We altered it to be a simple chat activity to be used in a webinar with hundreds of people attending. Going deeper, she took inspiration from computer scientist Alan Kay's quote, "Technology is anything that wasn't around when you were born."

SETUP

Design needs ahead of time: Create a slide asking participants to "List a technology that was not around when they were 10 years old."

Before the activity begins:

Facilitator: Review the years that make up the different generations, such as the Greatest Generation (1901–1943), Baby Boomers (1944–1964), Gen X (1965–1981), and Millennials (1982–2004).

Producer: Ensure that the chat is enabled and viewable by all participants.

THE ACTIVITY

SAY	DO
Facilitator: "Before we begin the webinar, and have a little fun, let's learn about who is here and how things have changed over the years. In the chat, list a technology that did not exist when you were 10 years old."	*Producer:* Help the facilitator by reading some of the answers out loud. *Facilitator:* Comment on the responses as appropriate. Enjoy!

Transition after the activity:

Facilitator: "As you know, technology changes very quickly, and as you can see, it is remarkable to see what did not exist when some of us were young. This certainly puts things into perspective!"

SPICE IT UP WITH THESE ALTERNATIVES

- Try an alternate question, such as, "What is the first rock or pop concert you attended?" This fun, simple question will likely reveal the generations of the people attending the webinar.
- For a training event, use a whiteboard. Ask participants to list 10 technologies that did not exist when they were 10 years old.
- For a breakout version, after asking people to brainstorm the list above, group them together and mix the generations to have a discussion on how things have changed and how that affects communication in the workplace.

In One Word

Purpose: To engage a large audience to use the whiteboard, by typing only a one-word response.

Session format: Webinar

Audience: Any

Number of participants: 100+

Time: 5 minutes

Materials: A slide

Features used: Share presentation, Whiteboard

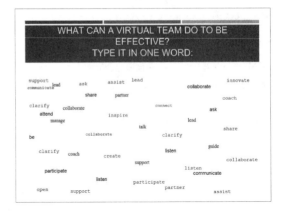

Description: Start this activity by creating a slide with enough space to type and include any directions as well. Ask participants to describe, in one word, what makes a virtual team effective.

If the audience is more than 50 people, try filtering the responses. Limit who will whiteboard by asking that only people who meet specific criteria add their answers to the whiteboard. For example, ask only those who have vacationed in Italy to whiteboard. Or ask those who are wearing green today to do it. Participants will truly love it. And it does not matter if they are not honest. During one webinar, we had four whiteboarding activities. By the fourth one, a participant sent a chat stating we had not yet chosen anything that applied to her. So we asked her to tell us where she had vacationed so we could use that for the next activity.

Backstory

Most webinar facilitators do not use whiteboarding activities. And for good reason: whiteboarding with more than 50 people can be a disaster. Why? The responses become illegible and undecipherable because people end up typing on top of each other's entries. To manage this, use In One Word combined with our idea of "filtering." We think you'll want to start adding at least one whiteboard activity to every webinar you deliver from now on.

SETUP

Design needs ahead of time: Create a slide that has the directions on what to respond to, using only one word.

Before the activity begins:

Producer: Ensure that the whiteboard tools is enabled, likely just for this activity.

THE ACTIVITY

SAY	DO
Facilitator: "We are going to be discussing the secrets of high-performing virtual teams today. To start let's use the whiteboarding tools to find out what you think a virtual team must do to ensure they are effective. If your birthday is in the month of August, please type your idea, using one word, on the whiteboard."	*Producer:* Provide direction on how to use the whiteboard tools, as needed. Save the whiteboard for reference later. *Facilitator:* Comment on the words participants have added to the whiteboard and relate it to the content of the presentation.

Transition after the activity:

Facilitator: "Based on all your words, you certainly know what virtual teams need to do to be effective. The question is, 'how do we ensure that this will actually occur?' Let's take a look next."

Conversation Starters

Purpose: To demonstrate key points through role playing.

Session format: Webinar

Audience: Any

Number of participants: 100+

Time: 10 minutes

Materials: A slide

Features used: Share presentation

Description: This activity is a classic role play, performed by the facilitator and the

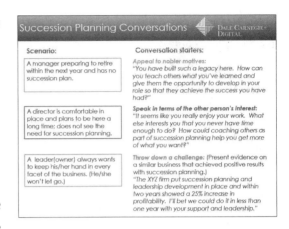

producer of the webinar, once the key techniques have already been covered. In the example here, the webinar topic is succession planning, and many ideas on how to approach succession planning within the organization have already been discussed. At this point in the webinar, this role play demonstrates how to manage a succession planning conversation with three specific people: a manager who plans to retire but has no plan in place, a director comfortable in her position who does not see the need, and a leader who wants to keep his hands in every facet of the business.

Make sure the slide is animated so that after the producer reads the role-play scenario, the facilitator will be able to read and explain the tip on how to have this conversation, in a way that would be motivating for each person and get the conversation started. Adjust the content to match the webinar topic, displaying the role-play scripts on the left for the producer to read, and then the response to it on the right. After each reading, encourage participants to react to what they noticed about the choice of words and tone used by the facilitator and producer.

SETUP

Design needs ahead of time: Create an animated slide with the appropriate examples of script for the facilitator and producer to read.

Before the activity begins:

Facilitator: Practice reading the role play out loud several times with the producer. Ensure that the slide is set up to be animated to reveal each item one at a time.

Producer: Practice reading the role play out loud several times with the facilitator.

THE ACTIVITY

SAY	DO
Facilitator: "We've covered several ways to manage succession planning within your organization, as well as ways to document your plans for follow up. Now it's time to have the important conversations with your leaders. Sometimes this can be challenging. We have prepared some examples and will role play them for you now.	*Producer:* Start the slide animation.
Producer: "I'm retiring a year from now. I don't have a succession plan in place; I'm not really sure I am ready to do that yet." *Facilitator:* "Appeal to nobler motives. You have built such a legacy here. How can you teach others what you have learned and give them the opportunity to develop in your role so that they achieve the success that you have had?"	*Facilitator:* Ask participants to comment on this approach in the chat. Respond appropriately.
Producer: "I'm not going anywhere just yet. Why the rush for a succession plan? Are you trying to tell me something?" *Facilitator:* "Speak in terms of the other person's interest. It seems like you really enjoy your work. What else interests you that you never have enough time to do? How could coaching others as part of your succession planning help you get more of what you want?"	*Facilitator:* Ask participants to comment on this approach in the chat. Respond appropriately.
Producer: "I'm the best person for this job. No one does it as well as I do." *Facilitator:* "Throw down a challenge. The XYZ Firm put succession planning and leadership development in place and within two years showed a 25 percent increase in profitability. I'll bet we could do it in less than a year with your support and leadership."	*Facilitator:* Ask participants to comment on this approach in the chat. Respond appropriately.

Transition after the activity:

Facilitator: "Thank you for your responses in the chat. These examples were also documented in your handout. Refer to them as much as you need."

Rewrite These (Version 1)

Purpose: To inspire an audience to actively demonstrate what they have learned.

Session format: Webinar

Audience: Any

Number of participants: 100+

Time: 10 minutes

Materials: A slide

Features used: Share presentation Chat

Description: This version of Rewrite These is

How would you turn these phrases around to be more motivating?

Jason is a poor time manager and consistently misses deadlines.

Ashley needs to improve her attitude to fit in better with the team.

Raj shows no follow-through and customers report that they don't like working with him.

a great activity because it can be done in many different ways. The basic idea is to provide participants with a poor example of the concepts being covered in the webinar so they have a chance to "rewrite" them according to the techniques learned. In this version, start by putting three statements on a slide, animated to come in one at a time to control which one participants are rewriting in the chat. Respond to the rewrites and read a few out loud, encourage participants to learn from one another, and then bring in the next one to repeat the process. Have the producer watch for questions, and encourage those who need help to raise their hand. The example here focuses on performance reviews, and before this activity, participants have learned many ways to deliver a motivating performance review to employees, even when the feedback employees need to hear is not easy to deliver. The statements on the slide are obviously not motivating, so it is up to the participants to rewrite them in a way that would be more effective and encouraging for the employee.

SETUP

Design needs ahead of time: Create a PowerPoint file with three poorly written statements.

Before the activity begins:

Facilitator: Review the statements and prepare a better way to say it to be ready with an example if necessary.

Producer: Ensure that the chat is enabled and viewable by all participants.

THE ACTIVITY

SAY	DO
Facilitator: "Now that we have discussed several techniques for delivering a motivating performance review, let's see how we would do when faced with some challenging yet very real situations. I am going to reveal, one at a time, statements from managers regarding difficult situations with three different employees. Each one has struggled with an issue I'm sure you can relate to: time management, attitude control, and lack of follow through. Write your rewrite in the chat."	*Producer:* Assist the facilitator by reading the chats and being prepared to read some out loud if requested. *Facilitator:* Read as many as you can as they come through. Once it slows down, start to read a few good ones out loud. Comment on them, look for questions, and then proceed through the next ones in the same manner.

Transition after the activity:

Facilitator: "Clearly, you have all paid attention throughout the webinar today. Your rewrites of these statements are motivating and encouraging. Way to go!"

Rewrite These (Version 2)

Purpose: To inspire an audience to actively demonstrate what they have learned.

Session format: Webinar

Audience: Any

Number of participants: 100+

Time: 10 minutes

Materials: Questions for multiple chat pods

Features used: Chat pods, Share pod for an image (optional)

Description: This Adobe Connect version

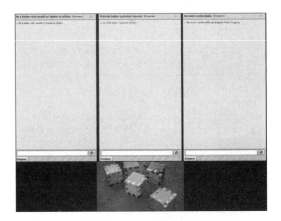

of Rewrite These is another example of how easily the chat pods can be used to engage a large audience to show what they have learned about the concepts discussed in the webinar. In this version 2, reveal all three items to be rewritten at once and let the participants choose which one (or ones) they want to rewrite. Give the participants a time limit (say, three minutes), and when the time is up, go back and focus on one at a time, reviewing the responses and commenting.

The example here uses the SMART process for writing goals. The webinar is about achieving success by setting realistic and measurable goals. Before this activity, participants have learned what SMART is, how it works, and how to write goals that follow the process. This activity provides a practice opportunity by allowing participants to choose which goal to rewrite.

To prepare this activity, simply create a new layout that includes three chat pods and a share pod for an image. The image is optional, but a nice touch for creating an engaging view. Label the top of each chat pod with a poorly written goal and arrange them in your layout in the way you like best.

SETUP

Design needs ahead of time: Determine what needs to be rewritten and label the chat pod accordingly. Choose a picture to load in a share pod to make the layout look more designed and visually pleasing (optional).

Before the activity begins:

Facilitator: Review the statements and be prepared to offer a better (rewritten) example of your own if necessary.

Producer: Ensure that the chat pods are labeled and ready to be used by all the participants.

THE ACTIVITY

SAY	DO
Facilitator: "Now that we have reviewed what makes a goal SMART and why we want that, let's take some time to consider how to rewrite some rather poorly written goals. These are unclear and could use some details to make them measurable. Take a look at the three chat pods and decide which one you would like to rewrite. When you are ready, enter your rewritten goal in the chat pod provided. We will take three minutes and then regroup and review all of them together."	*Producer:* Keep track of time, indicating when one minute remains and when the time is up. *Facilitator:* Read the rewrites as they come in and begin to prepare some comments.
Facilitator: "Thank you for all these responses! Let's take a look at the first one. I was reading through them as you were writing and you have made them much better: measurable and SMART."	*Facilitator:* Choose a few to read out loud and comment appropriately. Ask for clarification in the chat if needed.

Transition after the activity:

Facilitator: "Excellent! You are ready to write SMART goals and contribute more to the success and growth of your organization."

General Tips on Running Consistently Outstanding Webinars

This chapter, and this book more broadly, focuses on activities to drive increased participant engagement. But many other factors help drive engagement, and there's much more that goes into a great webinar than a string of activities. Here are some tips to help you produce outstanding webinars.

1. **Start with a "tour" layout or opening slide.** Because the webinar audience attendance could be large (100 participants or more), design the program with a "listen only" mindset. Participant introductions should be kept very brief, such as responding to one or two questions in chat, such as: "Where are you located?" or "What organization do you work for?" An alternative is to use a poll. This helps frame stories and give them context. The poll can be part of the tour or near the beginning of the actual webinar and help the facilitator get a sense of attendee opinions.

2. **Have the producer lead the tour or beginning.** Design the program so that the producer leads any tour activities, helps people with audio challenges, and reviews the communication tools. This allows the facilitator some time to read and reflect on the introductions and responses to any other chat or poll questions.

3. **Have the producer lead off the webinar itself.** When it is time to start the actual webinar, have the producer lead off and talk through the first few program slides (title slide, handout information, and producer and facilitator introductions). If webcams are used for introductions, the producer can go first and then turn it over to the facilitator. The facilitator and producer can also use an interview or dialogue approach throughout the webinar, and they can set the stage for this by building rapport during the initial introductions. It's important to note the producer will need to practice and hone his own presentation skills so the opening is high energy and impactful.

4. **Lead with a story.** In many cases the facilitator should lead with a story to build credibility with participants and answer the question, "What is my reason for being a subject matter expert on this particular topic?" The story should be one that creates high impact, and the facilitator should deliver it with some flair.

5. **Review objectives.** The facilitator should review the objectives for the webinar session, summarizing them but not reading them word for word. To get participants interacting during this summary, ask them to indicate which one is most important to them by entering it into the chat. (Be sure to number them so they can simply type the number rather than all the words.) This gives the facilitator insight as to what aspects of the program should be emphasized or de-emphasized.

6. **Check in with the audience early and often.** Ask the participants to say why they are attending the webinar. For example, ask, "Who works on a virtual team?" or "Who has ever struggled or felt uneasy when giving performance reviews?" Post such questions on a slide with a simple image and then ask participants to respond in the chat. During the webinar ask participants how they can use what they've learned in their organization or department. Relate their responses to the bottom line or goal of the session.

7. **Lead with data.** Depending on the nature of the first topic, some research data can help reinforce the importance of the topic, while setting the stage for the new concepts, processes, products, and other information that will follow.

8. **Get to the meat quickly.** If you are offering tips or recommended actions, offer at least some early in the webinar. Do not overload participants with a lot of background information, saving the key takeaways for the end. Instead, mix in the tips and recommended actions, and circle back to them as needed to reinforce them with more information, reasoning, and backstories. This is an important way to keep participants engaged rather than leading to frustration.

9. **Check in with your audience often.** Ask participants where they can use whatever you just showed them or did. Find out why the current topic may be important to them. What can they apply in their organization or department? Relate their responses to the bottom line or goal of the session.

10. **Remain conversational.** Throughout the webinar, remain as conversational as you can. Stay on script to make the key points—but don't sound scripted. Don't read from a manual or notes. Deliver the content naturally.

11. **Don't allow the technology to become the topic of your webinar.** After saying, "On screen you will see . . ." do not keep repeating it. Looking at the screen is an understood aspect of attending a webinar. Where else would your audience be looking? And after saying, "Type your ideas into the main chat," and establishing the chat as the main form of communication during the event, simply move on to saying, "Share your ideas." If there is ambiguity, clarify where they should type. Consider the program design and make sure it isn't overly complicated. Choose one way to communicate per direction to keep it simple and about the responses, not the technology used to respond.

12. **Reiterate the bottom-line benefits and give a call to action.** Before wrapping up the webinar, clearly reiterate the key points and benefits of the topic. In addition, give participants a call to action, such as "You've seen us do it. Now it's your turn." This will help ensure the webinar was time well spent.

13. **Debrief, discuss what's next, and close with an inspirational quote.** There are many ways to effectively close a successful webinar. Consider asking questions, such as, "What are your key takeaways?" and "What actions will you take?" If the webinar naturally leads to additional webinars, workshops, or in-person events, be sure to mention those. And closing with a quote and an impactful image is not only inspiring but also a great way to end on a high note.

Conclusion

Webinars pose unique challenges for facilitators to engage their large online audiences. Facilitators need a special focus and attention to storytelling, the pitch and tone of their voice, and the strengths of the technology platform to avoid delivering boring lectures. As this chapter has shown, well-designed webinars also include activities specifically designed for the potentially very large size of the audience. With the inclusion of such activities, it is very possible to engage an audience of hundreds or even thousands.

The next chapter provides activities that are geared toward online training events with a more intense learning focus and a smaller audience, where real coaching and practice are possible.

6

Lessen the Lecture: Engaging Virtual Training

. . . .

Virtual classroom training, virtual instructor-led training, synchronous online training—these are all names for live online training events that deliver interactive, collaborative, and impactful learning, either as a complement or substitute for traditional in-person classroom training or self-paced (asynchronous) e-learning courses. To fully define live online training events, let's contrast them with webinars, which were covered in the previous chapter.

Webinars are events for large audiences, usually more than 20 people, though they can grow to sometimes hundreds or even more than a thousand. They are commonly used for sales and marketing purposes, but they can be very effective learning events when their objectives relate mostly to knowledge and comprehension. Webinars focus on knowledge sharing, storytelling, and inspiration, and provide tools to use later; they do not focus on practice, live coaching, and learning that can be immediately assessed to test new skills.

In contrast, virtual classroom training events go beyond simply sharing knowledge; they often include application, analysis, synthesis, and evaluation objectives. These programs tend to have fewer than 20 attendees, allowing for robust coaching, practice of new skills, and if desired, assessment of these new skills. Multiple-session programs can include assignments or practical application between sessions, report-backs, time-spaced learning, and more.

Unlike webinars, virtual classroom training programs are robust learning events. It would be a mistake to run a webinar for a large audience and expect higher level objectives to be met. Just as it would be a mistake to run a virtual classroom training event as though it were a webinar with only knowledge- and comprehension-level objectives and still expect participants to remain engaged and walk away with lots of new skills.

Having explained the differences between webinars and virtual classroom training events, let's now also compare virtual classroom training with two other common formal training modalities: in-person instructor-led training and self-paced e-learning courses. See Table 6-1 for some of the pros and cons of each.

TABLE 6-1: PROS AND CONS OF THREE COMMON TRAINING MODALITIES

Training Type	Pros	Cons
In-person instructor-led training	• Rich coaching opportunities available from the instructor or other subject matter expert • Optimal way to role play and teach skills for some in-person behaviors • Comfortable learning modality because everyone has experienced it since childhood • Peer-to-peer, collaborative learning naturally occurs from well-designed programs • Social learning occurs naturally	• Physical location (classroom) required • All participants must be located in same area or travel to that location • Lack of ability to quickly gain rich input from all participants at once (only hand-raise level polling) • Sometimes somewhat less efficient to cover a given amount of material
Self-paced e-learning courses	• Available 24x7, from any computer (or increasingly, tablet or even smartphone) with an Internet connection • Participants can conveniently learn without leaving their office or home • No instructor or subject matter expert needed once the course is created • Comfortable learning approach for introverts • Comfortable learning approach for younger and tech-focused learners	• Often not very engaging resulting in little learning transfer and behavior change after the training ends, even when interactive activities are included • No live coaching from an instructor or other subject matter expert • No peer-to-peer, collaborative learning from the perspectives and experiences of other participants • No social learning element, unless complemented by discussion boards or other social media
Virtual instructor-led training	• Participants can be located anywhere with an Internet connection—no physical classroom location needed • Participants can conveniently learn without leaving their office or home • Ability to quickly gain rich input from all participants via synchronous text chat • Only effective way to teach and practice live online skills and behaviors • Comfortable learning approach for introverts, making it easier for them to contribute to the class • Comfortable learning approach for younger and tech-focused learners • Rich coaching opportunities available from the instructor or other subject matter expert • Peer-to-peer, collaborative learning naturally occurs from well-designed programs • Social learning occurs naturally	• Specific technology platform (such as Adobe Connect, WebEx, or others) and strong Internet connection required • Participants need at least minimal ability to use computers, a headset, and other tools • Unless webcams are used throughout, facial expressions and other in-person cues between participants are lost

TOPP Competencies for Live Online Trainers

So what makes well done live online training events so much more interactive, engaging, and impactful than self-paced e-learning courses and, in many cases, the equal of traditional in-person training? Well-designed and well-delivered activities. For live online training, including activities, to be delivered well, the facilitator must develop the unique training skills required to engage an online audience. The TOPP Competencies for Live Online Trainers we developed for Dale Carnegie Digital outlines the four areas every facilitator who wants to become an effective virtual trainer needs to master. As chapter 1 mentioned, TOPP stands for technical agility, on-air presence, preparation, and participant engagement.

Engaging virtual trainers are "technically agile," able to easily respond to the online learners who are communicating with raised hands, chat messages, and whiteboard entries. The technically agile trainer:

- attends to raised hands, chats, and whiteboard in a timely manner
- directs participants' attention to course materials, learning management systems, references, websites, and applications
- elicits support from producer when a participant needs assistance
- uses tools spontaneously and casually, while not letting them become the focus of the discussion
- informs participants when and how questions will be addressed
- offers participants alternative ways to successfully complete activities
- remains calm during unexpected situations and can manage on own if producer support is unavailable.

Second, trainers know their voices are their most important tool for maintaining engagement with an online audience. A trainer with a strong "on-air presence":

- speaks clearly and fluently to be understandable
- changes the tone and pitch of voice to captivate
- manages audio distractions, maintains appropriate volume, and eliminates background noise
- uses pauses appropriately and changes pace of speaking
- speaks with authority in a welcoming voice

- sounds enthusiastic to be delivering the session
- is webcam ready (wears professional attire, ensures proper lighting and neutral office background, and looks directly into the camera).

Third, trainers are just as prepared as producers to gracefully manage any possible challenges that may arise. A "prepared" trainer:

- uses the right equipment and computer for the platform (hard-wired Internet, landline phone, and approved headset)
- knows what to teach at the scheduled date and time—and clearly communicates any schedule changes that could affect program delivery
- downloads and reviews content in advance (studies it, researches it, and asks questions about it)
- conducts a thorough rehearsal within the platform with the producer well in advance of the live session
- is aware of backup plans and is prepared to implement them when needed
- researches and learns about participants' roles and industries by obtaining the roster in advance
- prepares examples and other evidence appropriate to the topic and audience.

And fourth, trainers drive the overall "participant engagement." To do this, the trainer:

- encourages others to answer questions instead of being the first to comment
- maximizes learning outcomes by asking clear, specific questions one at a time
- probes with questions that elicit deeper thought and responses from participants
- demonstrates empathetic level of listening rather than listening to respond
- goes beyond covering the prescribed content, and is able to make content relevant to participants so that they see the application to work situations
- encourages interaction, discussion, and collaboration, and provides clear directions to activities
- manages time and adheres to course objectives and flow, but can adapt to participant needs and expectations

But even with all of the TOPP Competencies mastered, without activities, live online training workshops can become too lecture heavy—two or more hours of low-impact, boring information dumps. They offer little or no engagement and collaboration and no coaching and practice. As a result, almost no long-term learning transfer, behavior change, and performance outcome improvement occurs. But live online training events don't have to be this way. The activities in this chapter, and others in this book, are ideally suited to engaging and motivating online learners.

One Word

Purpose: To break the ice on a topic, especially one that is controversial, challenging, or difficult to understand.

Session format: Training

Audience: Any

Number of participants: 5 to 25

Time: 5 minutes

Materials: A slide

Features: Slide used as whiteboard with annotation privileges enabled, Audio, Chat

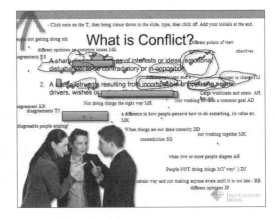

Description: This activity is quick and easy to facilitate with a larger audience. It is best to have participants respond through the chat, rather than directly on the whiteboard if the audience is larger than 16 participants. Try putting one word, specific to the training event, on a slide and asking the participants to define it. This activity can break the ice by addressing the elephant in the room immediately and getting people talking about their understandings and perspectives on a key concept or topic.

SETUP

Design needs ahead of time: Create a slide with the single word.

Before the activity begins:

Producer: Ensure that the slide is loaded. Ensure that whiteboard tools are enabled. Ensure that public chat is available.

THE ACTIVITY

SAY	DO
Facilitator: "As we are getting prepared for today's class, let's find out your experience as it relates to our topic of *[Insert class topic]*. "What is your definition of the word you see on this slide? Write it using your annotation tools, anywhere in the open space. Please mark the 'green check' when you are done."	*Producer:* Provide guidance on the tools as needed. *Facilitator:* Ask participants to respond through the chat if the audience is larger than 16.
Facilitator: "How do these insights affect our program topic *[Insert topic here]* today? How are we more, or less informed?"	*Facilitator:* Call on participants to explain their definition, while looking for similarities and differences. Encourage other participants to use their status indicators (laughter, applause, green check for agreement) as they listen.

Transition after the activity:

Facilitator: "Thank you for all your insights. Let's dive into *[insert class topic here]*."

Remember This?

Purpose: To sharpen the ability of participants to focus on details and recognize the
limitations of memory.

Session format: Training

Audience: Any

Number of participants: 5 to 15

Time: 5 minutes

Materials: Slides

Features: Slide used as whiteboard with
annotation privileges enabled, Audio, Chat

Description: Ask participants to try to describe everything they can remember about the
front side of a one dollar bill (or local currency, if an international audience), without
looking at it. Then present a slide that shows the one dollar bill, so participants can see
what they remembered correctly, what they missed, and what, if anything, they incorrect-
ly included that isn't there. You can then relate this exercise back to the training topic
(communications, sales, leadership, technology) in that you often take for granted things
that appear obvious or that you are used to seeing, but don't always remember what is
important and most relevant.

Backstory

I'd like to thank Abbe Hersing, instructional designer at Dale Carnegie Training, for
submitting this idea. This is my virtual classroom take on one of her favorite classroom icebreakers.

SETUP

Design needs ahead of time: Create two slides—one for whiteboarding and one with an
image of the front of a one dollar bill.

Before the activity begins:

Producer: Ensure that the first slide is loaded. Ensure that whiteboard tools are enabled. Ensure that public chat is available.

THE ACTIVITY

SAY	DO
Facilitator: "Without looking at a one dollar bill, describe what is on the front of a one dollar bill, and also what is on the back. Type your responses in the blank spaces on the whiteboard. Click on the *green check* once you are done."	*Producer:* Provide guidance on the tools as needed. *Facilitator:* Encourage discussion and comment on the responses. Ask participants to respond through the chat if the audience is larger than 16.
Facilitator: "Here is a picture of the one dollar bill. Let's examine what we missed or forgot to list—or what we imagined was there. Use the highlighter or circle tool, and use chat to mention things you thought were there but are not."	*Producer:* Display the next slide, showing the front side of a dollar bill. Provide guidance on the tools as needed.
Facilitator: "We often take for granted things that appear obvious and focus on things that are not important or irrelevant. [Relate this point back to the topic of the training program as appropriate.]"	

Transition after the activity:

Facilitator: "Now that we are paying close attention to detail let's take a look at *[insert class topic here].*"

SPICE IT UP WITH THESE ALTERNATIVES

- Use currency for the country of your audience.
- Bring up a logo for a product related to the training topic.
- Use any image relevant to your topic, industry, or company.

It's All About That Voice

Purpose: To demonstrate the importance that a speaker's voice has when presenting online or on the phone.

Session format: Training

Audience: Customer service representatives, online trainers, presenters, anyone presenting online

Number of participants: 2+

Time: 15 to 30 minutes

Materials: Slides

Features: Slides, Annotation tools, Chat, Audio

Description: To conduct this activity, simply present a slide with facial expressions. Try to select different expressions but do not include too many negative expressions. Adjust the images based on the culture of the audience attending the training. The facilitator should demonstrate the first example to break the ice. Choose a favorite and go overboard on play-acting it in order to set the tone. People often laugh and enjoy choosing which one it is either by guessing in the chat (if there are numbers next to each image) or by putting their pointers or any mark next to the one they think it is using their whiteboard annotation privileges.

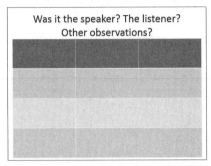

SETUP

Design needs ahead of time: Create one slide with a wide variety of facial expressions. Create a second slide that has a simple table grid so that participants can share insights and comments at the end of the activity (or use the chat feature.)

Before the activity begins:

Producer: Ensure that the first slide is loaded. Ensure that whiteboard and annotation tools are enabled. Ensure that public chat is available.

THE ACTIVITY

SAY	DO
Facilitator: "Can people really 'hear you smile'? In a virtual presentation, online training, or telephone conversation, it has been said that your voice is your most essential tool. Let's find out! "In front of you are images with different facial expressions. Some are happy, some are not so excited, and some are downright aggressive! What does the phrase, 'May I help you?' sound like when it is delivered in one of these *[number of images]* ways?"	
Facilitator: "Our volunteer's assignment is to deliver that line in one of these ways over the audio. The rest of us will use our whiteboard drawing tools to indicate which one we think it is. Please raise your hand to be the first volunteer." *Tip:* It is best practice to demonstrate this activity the first time yourself, before asking for a volunteer.	*Producer:* Provide guidance on the tools as needed. *Facilitator:* Listen to the volunteer. Encourage the others to use their tools to circle, check, or highlight the expression they think it is.
Facilitator: "Great job! Both in relaying the emotion of the expression, and in the rest of you guessing which it was. Who is the next volunteer?"	*Producer:* Erase all whiteboard annotations between volunteers. (Repeat these steps as many times as you would like, time permitting.)
Facilitator: "Well that was fun! Thank you to all the volunteers. I'm interested in what you think was happening here. Let's take a moment to analyze what we just experienced. "Was it the speaker's delivery that helped you uncover which emotion it was? Was it your own emotional intelligence or capacity to listen that helped guide you to the correct one? What other observations do you have? "Choose a spot on the grid and type your response. Type your name or use your pointer to identify your entry."	*Producer:* Load the grid slide. *Facilitator:* Ask participants to explain their responses. Encourage dialogue and comment appropriately.

Backstory

In her book *The Synchronous Trainer's Survival Guide,* Jennifer Hofmann details the importance of the live online trainer's voice: "In the synchronous environment, your voice is your most essential instructional tool." She could not be more correct, and I've experienced the lack of attention to voice, as I'm sure you have, to know there is no point in arguing about it! There's a limit to how long one will listen to a training workshop with a monotone presenter.

Karin Rex, owner of Geeky Girl, graciously gave me permission to share the voice skills activity in this book. This is by far my favorite activity for demonstrating the powerful effect voice can have on clearly communicating messages.

Transition after the activity:

Facilitator: "Thank you for your thoughtful comments and insights. I think we all would agree that when it comes to virtual presentations, live online training, and any telephone conversation we find ourselves having; our voice is our most important tool for conveying meaning in our message."

Do You Remember the Details?

Purpose: To have participants introduce themselves, and later test their memory on details about their peers.

Session format: Training

Audience: Any

Number of participants: 5 to 20

Time: Day 1: 10 minutes; Day 2: 5 minutes

Materials: 2 slides

Features: Slides used as whiteboards, Annotation tools, Chat, Audio, Webcams (optional)

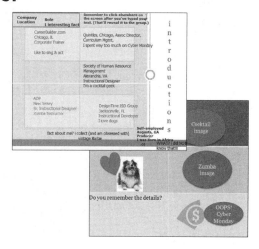

Description: This introductory activity is optimal for a two-day course. On Day 1, present a slide with a grid on a whiteboard that participants can use to introduce themselves. If the participants are known in advance, design the grid with each person's name already populated. (Even if someone does not show up, it's a nice touch to add a "hello, we missed you, enjoy the recording!" note for them in their box.) If not, participants can select any box by using a pointer or typing their name. Participants enter their name, company, location, role, and one interesting fact about themselves. Participants can speak about what they wrote; however, everyone doesn't need to speak because participants can read the whiteboard. The facilitator should comment on everyone's information and formally greet them even if they do not choose to speak up.

After Day 1, the facilitator should prepare the slide for Day 2 with the interesting facts located on another grid for the Do You Remember the Details? activity. Have some fun getting images to represent what people said—for example, an image of Africa for a participant who was born on the continent, or an image of a dog and a heart for one who loves dogs. The participants start the Day 2 session attempting to connect other participants with the details. There is often laughter, and it promotes discussion on just how much one remembers from the online classroom, without the nonverbal communication cues often present during an in-person training environment. This activity does not take long on Day 2, and it's a more natural result if participants aren't warned before the follow-up on Day 2.

Backstory

In the in-person classroom, we don't often have a record of introductions, unless we planned to make a videotape in advance or we assigned a person to take notes and record what is occurring. Every time I run an online class, I save the whiteboards and chats via a recording with all the participants' responses easily accessible. Using this information, you can create an activity to find out who remembers personal details about their fellow participants.

SETUP

Design needs ahead of time: For Day 1 create a slide with a grid that includes (optionally) the names of the participants and space for their information. For Day 2 create another slide filled with images representing aspects of each (or several) participants from Day 1.

Before the activity begins:

Producer: Ensure that the first slide is loaded. Ensure that whiteboard tools are enabled. Ensure that public chat is available.

THE ACTIVITY

SAY	DO
Facilitator: "Let's learn more about each other. In the box for your name, please indicate your name, company (if relevant), location, role, and one interesting fact about yourself."	*Producer:* Provide guidance on the tools as needed.
Facilitator: "Thanks everyone for sharing. Who would like to say a few words about themselves, perhaps to further explain the story behind their interesting fact?"	*Facilitator:* Comment on everyone's entries and formally greet them even if they do not choose to speak up. This is also how the balance of time is best managed.
Facilitator: On day two, "does everyone remember how we opened our session yesterday? Let's see how many of the details you remember. Based on the information shared yesterday, who is represented by each of the images shown? Enter names on the slide next to each image."	*Producer:* Ensure that the second slide is displayed. *Producer:* Provide guidance on the tools as needed.

Transition after the activity:

Facilitator: "Thank you for sharing yesterday, and for remembering so much about each other today. This demonstrates the power of live online learning—no one remembers everything from a training program, whether in-person or online, but if you are focused you can remember a lot. Now let's move on to *[new topic for Day 2]*."

Strategy Alignment

Purpose: To help leaders align business unit strategies with company strategy (or a similar purpose.)

Session format: Training

Audience: Functional Leaders

Number of participants: 5 to 20

Time: 20 minutes

Materials: A slide

Features used: Whiteboard, Audio, Timer

30 second elevator pitch to the CEO
How are you aligning the work of your team with the corporate strategy?

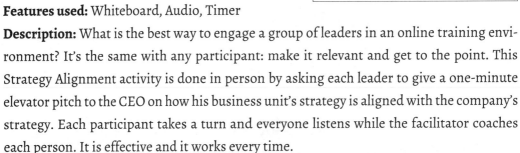

Description: What is the best way to engage a group of leaders in an online training environment? It's the same with any participant: make it relevant and get to the point. This Strategy Alignment activity is done in person by asking each leader to give a one-minute elevator pitch to the CEO on how his business unit's strategy is aligned with the company's strategy. Each participant takes a turn and everyone listens while the facilitator coaches each person. It is effective and it works every time.

To make this work efficiently and to be engaging online, simply change it from one participant at a time to a whiteboard activity for everyone, and then add a verbal activity for those who volunteer. Open by asking everyone to write a 30-second elevator pitch on the whiteboard and sign it. Let them know someone will be called on once they're done. Give them a time frame so it moves quickly and ask them to indicate when they are finished with a green check or a raised hand. The pitches can be one sentence, or just some keywords.

Ask them to read each other's pitches, and take a moment to review them and call on one person to give her pitch over the audio. Coach them, ask others to offer peer-to-peer coaching, and proceed for as long as everyone remains engaged and as time permits. Don't feel the need to cover all the participants because they learn from one another. Encourage participants to adjust their text on the whiteboard as they learn from each other.

SETUP

Design needs ahead of time: Create a slide with enough whiteboard space.

Before the activity begins:

Facilitator: Prepare an example. Type it on the whiteboard.

Producer: Ensure that whiteboard tools are enabled. Provide guidance on the tools as needed.

Backstory

I was in a planning meeting when someone suggested running this activity online with the 12 participants taking their turn on the phone. My response? "It won't work. Participants simply won't listen beyond the second or third pitch. They will check email instead." The team was surprised at first, but after I explained what would work, they understood. At the same time, I realized why designing live online training is so different from traditional in-person training. All participants should interact simultaneously during online activities, because taking turns, while everyone else waits, simply won't work. It's boring, and it takes too long. But with concurrent interaction and collaboration, everyone is engaged. As Dan Heffernan, vice president and general manager of Dale Carnegie Digital, said, "This is an example that cuts through the fog of why it is so different to take traditional instructor-led training and make it work online."

THE ACTIVITY

SAY	DO
Facilitator: "You're on an elevator with the CEO and she says to you, 'How is your business unit's strategy aligned with the company strategy?' You have 30 seconds to tell her, but here you have 2 minutes to write it. Use the whiteboard tools and sign it, and when you are done, click the *green check*."	*Producer:* Keep time and assist with the whiteboard tools if needed. *Facilitator:* Read the text as it appears, and prepare to call on someone.
Facilitator: "[Participant name], let's hear yours."	*Facilitator:* Coach and encourage peer-to-peer commenting and coaching as well. Proceed with a few more and encourage participants to make edits to their own whiteboard entry as the activity proceeds.

Transition after the activity:

Facilitator: "Not an easy task is it? Being very concise and precise in our language—whether spoken or written—is more difficult than writing longer documents or never getting to the point. Now let's apply what we've learned in this activity to *[next topic of the program]*."

Bingo! (for Training)

Purpose: To help participants minimize distractions by providing a reason to look and listen for key learning concepts.

Session format: Training

Audience: Any

Number of participants: 5 to 20

Time: Woven through the entire training event

Materials: A slide

Features used: Audio, Timer

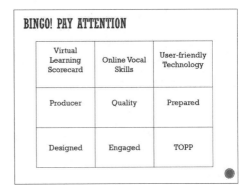

Description: What better way to keep people engaged than to give them a competitive game to play while learning? Trying to fill a bingo card with key learning concepts gives participants something to pay attention to instead of being tempted to email, use social media, or work on other projects. Create a table with words, phrases, numbers, or even images from the training event. Be sure to tell participants at the beginning of the session to be prepared to look and listen throughout the event. Have a bit of fun with this by asking participants to send a chat when they mark a square on their card. Once they have a complete row, column, or diagonal, encourage them to call out "Bingo!" just as they would at an in-person bingo game. Don't worry if it interrupts the session; it's supposed to be fun. As soon as they call it, have them explain each of the boxes, asking them to recall what they have learned regarding each topic.

SETUP

Design needs ahead of time: Create a bingo card related to the event. Add the bingo card to each participant manual, or email in advance if each participant needs to have a different one.

Before the activity begins:

Facilitator: Confirm that participants have located their bingo card, whether it is in the manual or has been sent to them in advance.

Producer: Email the bingo card (or participant manual) to anyone who needs one.

THE ACTIVITY

SAY	DO
Facilitator: "Take out your bingo cards and get ready to mark them. The topics we discuss today are on the card; when you first see it or hear it being discussed, mark your card and then feel free to send a chat too. When you have an entire row, call out 'Bingo!' The first person to call it out is the winner, but not before explaining each topic. Ready? Let's go!"	*Producer:* Enable the chat and make sure each participant has her bingo card. *Facilitator:* When a participant first proclaims "Bingo!", make sure he explains each of the items he connected—that helps all participants reinforce some learning from the program.

Transition after the activity:

Facilitator: "You got it! Great job explaining each of the topics. You win!"

SPICE IT UP WITH THESE ALTERNATIVES

You could run this same game activity during a larger webinar program, and perhaps give out a reward rather than have the participant debrief the concepts over the audio. Possible rewards, where relevant, include:

- a signed copy of a book
- a free live online training session/workshop pass
- gift cards to online sites
- early dismissal
- recognition later on an internal organization discussion board or other social media site
- recognition via email, copying in the participant's manager or team leader.

Website Scavenger Hunt

Purpose: Participants discover answers and report findings: on websites or in software, individually or in groups.

Session format: Training

Audience: Any

Number of participants: 5 to 20

Time: 20 minutes

Materials: Multiple slides

Features used: Share a slide, application, or desktop; Whiteboard; Audio; Breakouts (optional)

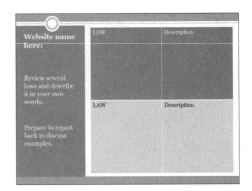

Backstory

Leslie Rawlins, instructional designer at Dale Carnegie Digital, said: "Scavenger hunts in live online training put the responsibility of learning directly on the participants. They can work alone, together in small groups, or teach each other in large group discussions—regardless, the activity allows them to solidly hit the course objectives. Participants are fully present, focused, and they're having fun." "It's a different and seldom used design approach, but designers and facilitators should really consider using scavenger hunts more often in their live online courses." I thought of this activity while working on a compliance training project for a global organization. We needed to develop a creative way for individuals to understand the U.S. laws regarding discrimination. Using a scavenger hunt model, I created an activity that would not only be engaging, but also be effective at helping managers apply the knowledge.

Description: This independent Website Scavenger Hunt activity works well when participants need to learn the key points and then remember the details as relevant situations arise. In this activity, each participant is assigned something to look up on a website and asked to answer a few questions. Time the activity and let participants know they will debrief their findings on returning to the main training session. This activity does not require formal breakout functionality in the technology. Simply send the link to the site in the chat, set a timer (or have the producer keep time), and be sure to list the questions in the participant manual for note taking.

SETUP

Design needs ahead of time: Confirm the website is active and accurate. Prepare the questions and present them on a slide, as well as in the participant manual for reference.

Before the activity begins:

Facilitator: Check the roster of participants. Plan what each person will research.

Producer: Enable chat. Check that the website is active.

THE ACTIVITY

SAY	DO
Facilitator: "In this next activity let's examine *[topic or aspects of a website resource]*. You will each be given an assignment. Please answer the questions found on page *[X]* of your participant manual. Then come back to our session and raise your hand when you are finished. Prepare to share your findings. You will have *[X]* minutes to find the answers to your questions.	*Producer:* Prepare assignments to send in chat. Send the link in chat. Keep track of the allotted time and call the participants back when it is time.
Facilitator: "Welcome back! Let's take some time and hear from each of you now. We'll start with the topic of *[one of the topics]*."	*Producer:* Help participants share their findings, as needed.

Transition after the activity:

Facilitator: "Excellent discussion! Let's now examine some situations where these laws are applied."

SPICE IT UP WITH THESE ALTERNATIVES

- Rather than having people communicate their answers as they are asked, prepare a whiteboard and have participants type their findings using the annotation and whiteboard tools. Debrief by asking for volunteers or calling on participants with specific questions for more detail.

- Share the screen to the website during the debriefing if showing a visual helps. Highlight it with your cursor while calling on participants to talk about what they learned. Alternatively, pass the presenter rights to the participant.
- For team versions, use breakout sessions, assign several topics to each team, and request that the team prepare to report key ideas after a specified time in the breakout. Have them prepare their key findings on a whiteboard that is shared with the main training session on their return (see chapter 9 for more on using breakouts).
- Here are some other scavenger hunt examples:
  - Marketing example: Use breakout groups and have teams research competitor websites. They can share their screens to the websites in the breakout, document their findings, and prepare to report back to the other groups when finished.
  - Software example: Provide a list of features to discover in a software program. Have participants document the correct steps to complete an action performed using the software.
  - Human resource example: Give participants a list of benefits to research and learn more details by searching the company intranet.

Make the Connections

Purpose: To assess what participants have learned by letting them put it into their own words.

Session format: Training

Audience: Any

Number of participants: 5 to 20

Time: 10 minutes

Materials: A slide

Features used: Share a slide, Whiteboard, Audio

Description: If for some reason you were only permitted to run one activity in an online training event, this Make the Connections activity is a prime candidate. Fun to plan, design, and facilitate, it provides valuable insight into learner understanding, and participants always have a good time. The example here is one designed for an auto insurance company and used during the training of new agents. There are three columns representing a client who could walk through the door or call at any time. The first column is the people, the second is the type of car they own, and the third is where they reside. Ask each training participant to choose an image from each column and then describe the auto insurance plan they would recommend for that client. For example, a family of four who owns a minivan and lives in a city: What insurance package is most appropriate for them? Simply have training participants use their whiteboard tools to place a circle around their selection and then unmute their audio to describe the package and their reasoning. Ask clarifying questions, probe for more details, and provide additional coaching as needed.

SETUP

Design needs ahead of time: Prepare a slide with three columns and three rows of images.

Before the activity begins:

Producer: Load the slide. Ensure that whiteboard tools are enabled.

THE ACTIVITY

SAY	DO
Facilitator: "In this review activity, you will construct a scenario by choosing images—one from each column—and then describing an approach or solution from that combination. When it is you turn you will use the whiteboard tools to circle your chosen images. Do I have a volunteer to go first?" [If no one immediately volunteers, it could be that they are unsure of what is being asked of them. Do a quick example yourself to model what you are looking for.]	*Producer:* Assist participants with the whiteboard tools, as necessary. *Facilitator:* Allow each person to take a turn, coaching on the content and solutions as needed.

Transition after the activity:

Facilitator: "Nice work describing [the solutions] as you would to new clients. Practice makes better, but I'm confident each of you are ready to go!"

SPICE IT UP WITH THESE ALTERNATIVES

- For nurse training, have participants identify various medical instruments used in different situations and why.
- For a new hire orientation, use pictures that represent departments and processes. Allow new hires to make the connections on how they interact and with whom.
- Use pictures of technology, and ask participants to tell the story of how each part works and what it is used for.
- For B2B Sales training, have participants determine which product or solution is best for various types of businesses facing different types of challenges.

Recognizing Diversity

Purpose: To set a baseline definition for a word or concept.

Session format: Training

Audience: Any

Number of participants: 5 to 20

Time: 10 minutes

Materials: 3 slides

Features used: Share a slide, Whiteboard, Chat, Audio

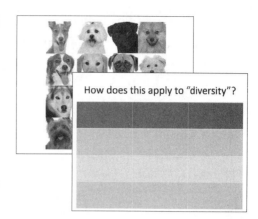

Description: This Recognizing Diversity activity requires three slides. The first slide explains to participants that they will soon hear a word (such as "dog") and that they should close their eyes and create a mental image of it. Ask them to close their eyes and focus on it for one minute.

Toward the end of the minute, move to the second slide that has images of the "word" all over it (in the example here, the second slide shows many different breeds of dogs). Allow a few moments for participants to mark the pictures that are most similar to what they thought about and then to discuss what they were thinking and why. Ask what is different and also what is similar.

The third slide is a table with a question such as: "What is your definition of diversity?" Debrief by making the point that people have varied beliefs, backgrounds, and experiences that shape their lives and who they are. Everyone sees the world differently.

Backstory

It's easy to assume training participants are all on the same page with a concept or a definition. This Recognizing Diversity activity reminds trainers to take a step back and confirm participants' understanding before proceeding to further compliance explanations or guidelines on company standards. Lena Hull, HR Trainer at the VyStar Credit Union, shared this "level set," and I not only learned from it, but I also enjoyed participating, even if I would have preferred she used cats instead of dogs.

SETUP

Design needs ahead of time: Create one slide that explains the directions and reveals the chosen word or concept. Create a second slide that shows pictures of the word or concept. Create a third slide that has a table with a question for participants to whiteboard their answers.

Before the activity begins:

Producer: Ensure that the whiteboard tools are enabled. Ensure that public chat is enabled.

THE ACTIVITY

SAY	DO
Facilitator: "To start let's do a visualization exercise. In just a moment, I'm going to give you a word, and when I do, you'll have one minute to close your eyes and create a mental image of it. Remember to keep your eyes closed. The goal is for you to see the object in your mind. We're going to go ahead and get started now. The word is *[chosen word]*."	*Producer:* When the minute is almost up, switch to the second slide.
Facilitator: "Time is up. Go ahead and open your eyes. Now let's take a look at some pictures of *[chosen word]*. "As you can see, there are many different types represented here. Using your checkmark tool, indicate which one most closely resembles the mental image you had in your mind."	*Producer:* Call time after one minute. Enable annotation tools. Provide assistance as needed. *Facilitator:* Give the participants a moment to mark their selections.
Facilitator: "It looks like you had many different ideas about what a *[chosen word]* looks like. What are some factors that you think could have caused us to have such different responses? Please chat your responses."	
Facilitator: "We're going to take a moment now to discuss how what we just did relates to diversity. "Using your pointer tool, claim a space on the whiteboard, and then share at least one way that the visualization exercise we just did can be applied to the idea of diversity. Take about two minutes, and when you're done, please mark the 'green check.'"	*Producer:* Switch to the third slide. Provide assistance with the whiteboard tools, as necessary.

Transition after the activity:

Facilitator: "As we can see, we are all very diverse. We have different beliefs, backgrounds, and experiences that shape our lives and who we are. We all see the world differently. Let's examine this further in our next activity."

SPICE IT UP WITH THESE ALTERNATIVES

- Change the pictures.
- Change the word or concept.
- Change the debrief question.

Enjoy the View!

Purpose: To have some fun while getting significant practice working with the whiteboard drawing tools, chat, and breakout rooms.

Session format: Training

Audience: A new team or an existing team

Number of participants: 5 to 15

Time: 15 minutes

Materials: 6 slides, a poll, a reward

Features: Breakouts, Slides used as whiteboards with annotation privileges enabled, Audio, Chat, Webcam (optional)

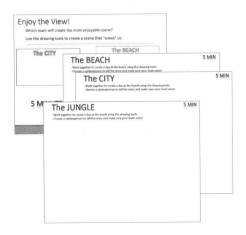

Backstory

More than once, I have been asked to facilitate a live online training event with 50 to 100 people attending. With such larger numbers, the opportunity to collaborate becomes challenging due to time, technical issues, and platform restrictions. This Enjoy the View! activity was born out of my refusal to deliver a boring lecture, even though it was going to be challenging not to. I'm always surprised at how well this goes because I assume people need to talk in order to work together. But the truth is sometimes they just don't need to. The drawings are always amazing and the stories behind them are collaborative, funny, and thoughtful.

Description: Introduce the activity as a bit of creative competition during which participants will work together to draw one of three scenes—only chatting, no talking. Place the participants in one of three groups, using the feature in breakouts in which groups are automatically distributed among the number of rooms created, which makes the activity faster and easier to facilitate. Once the breakouts begin, the participants will see which group they have been added to once they join their breakout and view the slide that has been prepared for them. Ensure the drawing tools are on, keep track of time, and wait for the fun to happen. Encourage those who are concerned about their drawing ability to go beyond their comfort zone—they always create something they thought they couldn't.

With 30 seconds left, send a broadcast breakout message to the teams, reminding them to choose a spokesperson to tell the story of their scene. End the breakouts and bring them all back. Show the pictures, and allow a volunteer from each team to debrief the scene, encouraging them to make it memorable so they can get the most votes. This activity is fun and doesn't require too much explanation to make it a success.

SETUP

Design needs ahead of time: Create one slide that explains the directions. Create a second slide with an image to represent voting. Create a third slide with the reward, which can be whatever is best suited to the audience. Create three separate slides for the breakout rooms with plenty of space for the groups to draw their scenes (see the examples in this activity).

Before the activity begins:

Producer: Ensure that the whiteboard tools are enabled. Confirm that the beach, city, and jungle slides are loaded into three breakout rooms. Ensure that public chat is enabled. Ensure that a poll is ready and loaded that asks participants to choose either beach, city, or jungle. Have a timer to keep track of time.

THE ACTIVITY

SAY	DO
Facilitator: "So in this next activity, we are going to have some fun through competition, while also testing your drawing skills! On the screen you see three boxes labeled 'Beach,' 'City,' and 'Jungle.' You will be challenged to draw one of these scenes."	*Producer:* Prepare the three breakout rooms. Use the breakout feature to automatically distribute the participants evenly.
Facilitator: "Which team will create the scene that is the 'most enjoyable' to view? Using your drawing tools and only chat to communicate, work together to draw your chosen scene. The trick? You cannot talk—you may only chat and use the drawing tools. After three minutes we will ask you all to 'put your pencils down' and have a volunteer tell us the story of your scene. We will then vote on which one was most enjoyable. Questions? Raise your hand at any time. "All right, *[producer]* will now explain how you get to your scene and start drawing!" *Producer:* "Sure, thanks *[facilitator]*! You will be transferred into one of three groups: the beach, the city, or the jungle. You will know once you enter your breakout room. Use the drawing tools to collaboratively create your scene! I'll keep time. Raise your hand if you have questions, and have fun!"	*Producer:* Start breakouts and assist participants to navigate to their breakout room and with the drawing tools as necessary. Start a timer. Provide a 30-second warning reminding them to select a volunteer to talk about their scene. Call "time" after three minutes and end the breakouts. Bring the three scenes into the main viewing area.
Facilitator: "Welcome back everyone! Let's regroup and hear from a volunteer for each group. Tell us about your scene and why we should vote for it. Beach team—you're up first."	*Facilitator and Producer:* Comment on each of the three drawings, and respond to the volunteer's story.
Producer: "OK, so let's run the poll to see who has won this competition."	*Producer:* Open and run the poll, and then close it when ready. Share the results.
Facilitator: "Congratulations *[winning team]*! You all did a great job using the drawing tools. What did we learn in doing this? What questions do you have?"	

Transition after the activity:

Facilitator: "Well that was fun! Now that we have set the tone for some competition and quick drawing skills, let's see what we have in store for you next!"

SPICE IT UP WITH THESE ALTERNATIVES

- Don't use breakouts:
    - For WebEx, turn on the attendee privilege to "view any document" and load the beach, city, and jungle files as separate presentations. They will be tabs at the top of the meeting window. Ask participants to click on the scene of their choice. Keep track of time and then, as presenter, click to the tabs at the top to debrief. As presenter, you bring the whole group with you.
    - For Adobe Connect, load the files into three separate share pods, in one layout. Make them as big as you can and tell each person to click to the *share pod/scene* that is their group. Let them choose, or assign them. Everyone will see each other's, but that is OK because it is a quick activity.
- Change the drawings to anything applicable to your organization, event, topic, or audience.

Virtual Training as Social Learning

For almost a decade now the learning and development industry has been abuzz with talk of "social learning." Countless magazine articles, blog posts, and conference presentations have urged training managers and chief learning officers that they need to start using social media technologies to enable more social learning in their organizations—or risk losing the attention of Millennials or otherwise be left behind the curve of a major trend. The rest of this chapter will examine this phenomenon, and suggest an alternative way to approach the desire to focus on social learning in organizations—one that leverages virtual classroom technologies as part of the toolkit.

WHAT IS SOCIAL LEARNING?

Various definitions of social learning have been put forward in recent years. Here's ours: social learning is learning through interactions with others and through the knowledge and expertise of others. A nice, simple definition, but one that does not include too much or too little. After all, many instances of learning are social, but not all: the child who touches a hot stove and quickly learns that this will burn his fingers; a computer programmer who uses trial and error to figure out how to write a program to accomplish her goal; or someone who goes for a walk in the woods, and learns which birds make each kind of bird call.

There are four types of social learning: one-to-one, one-to-many, many-to-one, and many-to-many. Let's consider examples of each in turn (Figure 6-1).

FIGURE 6-1. FOUR TYPES OF SOCIAL LEARNING

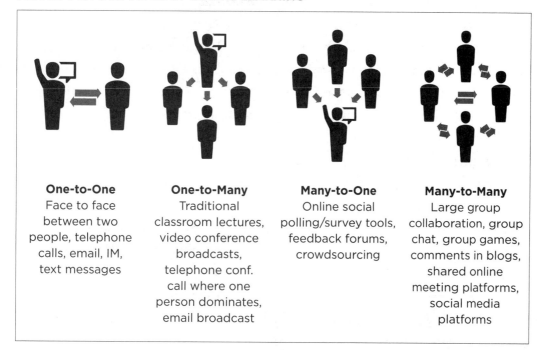

One-to-One	One-to-Many	Many-to-One	Many-to-Many
Face to face between two people, telephone calls, email, IM, text messages	Traditional classroom lectures, video conference broadcasts, telephone conf. call where one person dominates, email broadcast	Online social polling/survey tools, feedback forums, crowdsourcing	Large group collaboration, group chat, group games, comments in blogs, shared online meeting platforms, social media platforms

A parent teaching a child how to ride a bicycle, a personal trainer showing how to lift weights properly, a colleague demonstrating the proper way to enter data into an accounting application—these are all examples of the first type of social learning, one-to-one. In each case one person is learning from another, from their knowledge and expertise. While some in the learning field don't readily consider the transfer of knowledge between two people, such as personal coaching and mentoring, to be social learning, it is.

Expanding the audience for teaching or instruction beyond one recipient describes the traditional model of classroom learning—whether grade school, university, or corporate in-person instructor-led training events. This second type is social because the learning is through interactions with others, and through the knowledge and expertise of others. Again, while traditional lectures might not seem particularly social, such one-to-many examples are still important forms of social learning and can be very effective in many contexts.

The third type of social learning—many-to-one—is the inverse of the traditional lecture. Examples here include polls, surveys, and other attempts to crowdsource information from several, hundreds, or millions of people. Whether gathering information for analysis, determining the range of opinions, or asking for advice on a problem—in each case learning occurs through interactions with others and from the knowledge and expertise of others. Such cases of many-to-one learning are not often immediately thought of as social, but they too fit the definition.

The fourth type of social learning—many-to-many—is what most learning and development professionals have been conditioned to regard as social learning. Many-to-many social learning includes large group collaboration events, active classroom training with a good deal of discussion and peer-to-peer activities, most learning-based gamification, and online discussion forums and meeting spaces. They can be very powerful, partly because of their dynamism, lack of structure, and unpredictability.

Social learning—whether one-to-one, one-to-many, many-to-one, or many-to-many—is not new. Rather, it has been around for millennia, and will continue as long as there are humans learning.

While it isn't correct to call social learning a fad or trend, attention to it has been trending upward in recent years. In particular, learning professionals have been seeking ways to enable more social learning in their organizations. Ramping up peer-to-peer interaction in instructor-led in-person classroom events is one possibility. But new technologies can also play a role.

WHAT IS SOCIAL MEDIA?

As with social learning, let's start with a clear, simple definition. According to Merriam-Webster, social media refers to "forms of electronic communication (as Web sites for social networking and microblogging) through which users create online communities to share information, ideas, personal messages, and other content (as videos)." Books, magazines, newspapers, movies, and television shows are forms of media, but on their own are not social media. Even traditional, one-way informational websites or computer software are not social media, because their purpose is not to enable users to create and share content or to participate in social networking.

So what does count as social media? Many people use the "I know it when I see it" approach, which often leads to mentions of Facebook, LinkedIn, Twitter, YouTube, and others. But these popular platforms are not the end of it. There are the social media features of broader websites, such as the rating and review features at Amazon.com and other e-commerce sites, or the literally millions of online discussion forums, blogs, and wiki-based sites. All are examples of social media.

What about in the workplace? Social media can serve a wide range of purposes for communication, collaboration, and learning and development. Most consumer-based social media have had similar versions intended for business purposes. Some have been smashing successes; others have launched with great excitement only to fade away. Popular tools include Yammer and SalesForce Chatter, which can increase collaboration and idea sharing, improve customer service response times, and enable more and higher quality social learning.

The learning and development industry has seen a great many social media features added to learning management systems and other business applications. These include features that make it easy to post and comment on videos (like YouTube), maintain a profile and update one's status (like Facebook and Twitter), write short essays and opinion pieces (like WordPress and Blogger), rate and review formal training content (like Amazon ratings and reviews), ask questions and give answers (like consumer discussion forums), and crowdsource the development and sharing of vast archives of information (like Wikipedia). Most of the largest, widely used learning management systems now provide modules that include some or all of these social media features.

When designed or used poorly, these features can lead to significant wastes of time and money. But when used with the right mix of vision, strategy, and freedom, they can greatly enhance traditional organizational learning solutions (Figure 6-2). They do this most of all by enabling greater social learning than what would otherwise occur in a classroom or from the informal day-to-day interactions among colleagues.

Unlike social learning, which is not new, these powerful social media tools are. And for all its benefits, social media still raises many concerns that lead it to be barred in some organizations as a tool to enhance learning. Notable are privacy or security concerns and information control objections. These concerns make it difficult for learning and development professionals interested in social media to test, let alone roll out, such technologies to enable greater social learning. But what if there were technologies—ones that the organization has already bought into for other purposes—that could be leveraged to enable more social learning? Technology that rarely if ever faces these same kinds of political and other hurdles?

FIGURE 6-2. THE OVERLAP OF SOCIAL LEARNING AND SOCIAL MEDIA HOLDS GREAT PROMISE

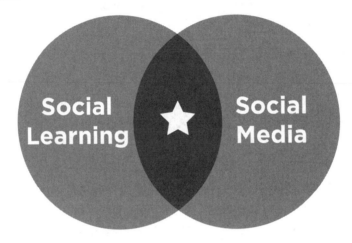

Even in organizations that have not faced, or have managed to overcome, such challenges to social media, consider this additional reason to look for another approach. How many social media features and tools used in workplaces are essentially asynchronous? How many enable information sharing, collaborating, and social learning but with varying gaps between the times of interaction? While this allows workers to participate with and learn from others when it is most convenient and after they have had time to reflect on the questions or answers, it lacks the efficiency and power of having live conversation with others.

So which learning and development technologies can fill this gap—by assuaging security and control concerns while enabling more synchronous social learning? Virtual classroom technologies like Adobe Connect and WebEx.

VIRTUAL CLASSROOMS CAN ENABLE MORE SOCIAL LEARNING

Adobe Connect, WebEx, and similar technologies used for learning are most commonly thought of as platforms for formal learning programs: training that involves a curriculum, with learning objectives, led by an instructor—a sage on the virtual stage. This kind of learning is already social, even when it amounts to nothing more than a one-way lecture. But how can virtual classroom technology be used to enable more social learning, especially many-to-many forms of social learning? Through robust, well-designed, synchronous activities. There are several keys to getting this result. Let's consider each in detail.

Redesign for Interactivity and Collaboration

To enable greater social learning through virtual classroom technologies, one has to go back to the training program's design. Was it developed creatively and with this goal clearly in mind? Did the instructional designer simply create a PowerPoint slide deck rich with content to be lectured to attendees? Or was some thought put into how to make the learning event more interactive—for example, by using activities like those in this book? There is a big difference between a typical lecture-style event and a highly interactive live online training program.

Going beyond greater interactivity—to really kick the engagement level and the social learning opportunities into high gear—requires truly collaborative activities. They need to go beyond simply asking and answering questions in the chat or using polling features. The activities in this book, and the many others being used in robust live online training every day, generate not just a single response from most or all participants, but get participants truly conversing with each other, building on each other's responses and ideas, and working together to brainstorm, prioritize, and categorize. Collaboration is a great way for virtual training participants to learn more socially. It is a key feature of well-designed in-person classroom activities, so virtual classroom events should strive to reflect this as well.

Set the Social Stage

Even a well-designed virtual classroom event can fail to reach its goals if participants are not properly prepared. Participants need to be ready to engage, collaborate with each other, and learn together, not multitask or catch up on email.

To make sure that they are ready, the social stage must be set. First, participants need to know ahead of time what experience to expect. Event announcements, enrollment emails, and even short recorded videos can all promote the interactive and collaborative features of the upcoming event. Giving participants a heads-up that the event will differ from what they are used to can go a long way in enabling greater social learning in the virtual training program.

Second, as participants arrive in the virtual training room, give them plenty to do right away. Show a tour slide that introduces the key features they need to know about to help reduce any anxieties about technology they may have. Ask a poll question to get them interacting, and have a dedicated chat area with either "get to know you" questions or an initial question related to the program's topic. (See chapter 2 for details on the tour concept and other activities to start your program.) Facilitators and producers need to be very active during these early moments of the program, making sure everyone is getting connected, encouraging conversation either through audio or text chat, and noting responses to the poll. Doing so sets the social stage and makes clear to participants that they will not be able to multitask during the virtual training program the way they did in yesterday's webinar.

Whiteboard Is a Verb

"Whiteboard" in a traditional sense is mostly commonly used as a noun. In a physical classroom it's that glossy, white-colored replacement for the old green- or black-colored chalkboards. In the virtual classroom it's often the name of a platform feature: a blank white area where participants can add text or draw various shapes.

But "whiteboard" can also be used as a verb—and should be treated as such when designing live online training events. To whiteboard is the act of adding text or drawing shapes in a virtual classroom. This could be on the whiteboard feature, but it could also be on a PowerPoint slide—for example, a slide designed for the express purpose of asking participants to "whiteboard their responses," "whiteboard a list of ideas," or "whiteboard what the solution might look like."

Many of the activities in this book involve and emphasize "whiteboarding" activities as a critical way to get learners to engage with the content and collaborate with each other.

The more you think of whiteboard as a verb—whether as an instructional designer or as a virtual trainer—the more the live online program is likely to enable social learning.

Create a Chatversation

Using whiteboard as a verb expands your vocabulary, and so does introducing a new concept: a "chatversation," or a robust, free-flowing learning conversation that develops in well-designed and well-delivered virtual training events. Far too many virtual trainers are concerned that the chat feature in the virtual classroom will distract their participants. They fear that learners will not be able to hear or keep up with the important content being taught. While understandable at first, the issue passes with enough practice and comfort with the tools. The problem isn't the chat; it's that virtual trainers are not yet skilled enough to leverage this wonderful tool.

Some trainers use the chat only at specific points in their virtual training programs, hiding it or turning it off when they aren't directing participants to respond to a question. This degrades the chat tool to being little more than the poll feature. If instead the chat feature is left open throughout the program, learners can ask questions through it, respond to each other, encourage each other, and more important, engage in a powerful new learning opportunity—the chatversation. It enables many-to-many style social learning in the virtual classroom.

Chatversations are difficult, if not impossible, to foster to the same degree in a traditional classroom. Consider a physical classroom with 20 people. The instructor can ask a question, but typically only get one response at a time, perhaps controlling it through the raising of hands or the like. If Mary in the front row has a question, she can ask the instructor—but can't as easily ask the rest of the class without interrupting what the instructor is saying. That is, she can't easily get a response from Cheryl in the third row, or Peter in the back row, let alone several people all at once. But with a lively chatversation in a virtual training event, this kind of peer-to-peer, many-to-many social learning happens naturally and leads to far more learning than would otherwise occur.

Objections to open chatversations revolve around training contexts in which participants might not act appropriately if given so much freedom to interact or if the content of the training is highly sensitive, open to misinterpretation, or in need of some measure of control. While perhaps valid, they aren't good reasons for ending the chatversation entirely. A continuum of freedom and control should be considered, with some constraints to rein in people only if they go far off topic, give out false information, or act inappropriately. In fact, this important role can be filled by the producer, monitoring the chatversation and keeping it alive if it seems to dwindle.

Another tip, provided to us by Jimmy Bayard, facilitation manager at Best Buy, is to encourage the more experienced participants, or the subject matter experts in the program, to change their text color to a selected color that will represent them. This way their text messages will stand out from the rest, raising awareness that what they are saying is more likely to be valuable and worth reading amidst the streaming conversation.

Combine the Virtual Classroom With Social Media

Social media can enable greater social learning in an organization—when used well. The best approaches typically avoid the "If you build it, they will come" mentality that many in the learning and development field followed in the early days of Web 2.0 and social media tools. Some design and structure is necessary. But imposing too many restrictions on the how, why, and when aspects of using social media can lessen its benefits. So, like many things in business and life, reasonable goals coupled with some measure of freedom will bring the best results—and in this context increase the social learning opportunities for learners.

Combining asynchronous social learning enhanced by social media with synchronous social learning enhanced by virtual classroom technologies can achieve far more than each practice on its own. Why? Blended learning programs maximize the power of all the tools at your disposal.

Consider a program that centers on two, 2-hour live online training events. Before the first event, participants respond to some provided questions in a discussion forum or in a cohort group set up in a tool such as Yammer or Chatter. They attend the first live online event, which is designed to include whiteboard activities, robust chatversation, and breakout activities. After the first event, they are asked to read a blog post and react to it in the comments section of the post. Meanwhile, asynchronous conversation continues in the cohort group, using Yammer, Chatter, or a similar status updating tool. The participants later attend the second live online event, which starts with some reflection and discussion of the blog post. The event is also designed for social learning, with whiteboard activities and robust chatversation. After the training program wraps up, conversation and learning continue in the discussion forum (or other tool), helping participants transfer learning to their regular jobs.

Now, consider this alternate approach, one that places social media tools at the center. Participants join a discussion forum or a Yammer or Chatter conversation group and respond to provided questions or topics. As conversation and learning develop, the trainer acts as the moderator, or "gardener," pruning any tangents and watering the conversation to keep it alive if it starts to slow. After a few weeks of meaningful dialogue and learning, the trainer schedules two, 1-hour targeted learning events to address some issues that would benefit from synchronous brainstorming and collaborating. The first event is a brainstorm session to come up with possible solutions to the issues. The second event is a more formal technical training session to address the issues. After the events, the participants communicate asynchronously in discussion forums or through other such social media tools, by prioritizing the items brainstormed from the first event and by discussing related topics and continuing to learn from each other.

Conclusion

Just as online meetings and webinars can be greatly improved through the use of well-designed activities, virtual training programs will be far more interactive and engaging with robust activities included. Well-designed activities used appropriately in a training program will transform it from a series of lectures into a rich learning experience that is more likely to produce the kind of skill development and behavior change desired. In addition, activities in the virtual classroom can be a great addition to your strategy for enabling more social learning in your organization.

7

Leave a Lasting Impression: Close With Impact

· ·

One of the biggest mistakes made in an online event is failing to leave enough time to properly bring the session to a close with a memorable wrap-up activity. Planning a closing activity for the online event will leave a lasting impression, one that ensures that the time spent in the event was well worth it. The activities in this chapter engage participants to contribute their own thoughts and ideas on how they'll take the knowledge and skills learned in the online event into their own environments.

Before reviewing the activities, let's address the elephant in the online room: the concept of "on time" has seemingly lost its importance since the onset of the technology to meet live online. Starting and ending on time is unfortunately not the norm. From the technical challenges at the beginning to long lectures from presenters to the lack of attendee participation, closing well and on time is no longer a priority. The more common reaction at the end is "I survived this so let's get out of here as fast as possible"; rather than taking the time to thoughtfully close with proper debriefings, wrap-up comments, and action items. Surely it's time to change this.

Here are five surefire ways to end a meeting, webinar, and live online training on time:

- **Start on time.** Do not wait to start until all participants arrive. Late participants can catch up, and most people do not want to be singled out for having arrived late. Give participants the benefit of the doubt and remember we all lead busy lives and intend to be on time to all appointments. Start on time to end on time.

- **Control the tangents.** Once participants start to discuss the material, it's a challenge to figure out how much time to allow them to continue. Pay close attention to the conversations. Guide them on topic and to action with efficiency. Put a halt to tangents and schedule them for another time, perhaps on asynchronous discussion boards or in follow-up meetings.

- **Watch the clock.** Have a designated timekeeper. Plan the time in advance and pay attention to how long it takes to make each point. If some take too long, find a more efficient way to get to the point the next time.

- **Plan the activities.** Plan for them to change as participants perform the actions of those activities. Always stay alert by listening to the needs of the participants. They expect feedback with openness and flexibility, but they too do not want to be online past the scheduled end time.

- **Examine the process.** If the online event does not end on time, review why it ran long in order to improve for your next event. Reflect on the event, watch the recording, take notes, and review the previous. What went well? What can be improved? Take action.

Questions in the Jar

Purpose: To assess what participants have learned by having them take turns to answer questions.

Session format: Training

Audience: Any

Number of participants: 4 to 16

Time: 30 minutes

Materials: A PowerPoint file

Features used: Share PowerPoint presentation, Audio, Breakouts

Description: This Questions in the Jar activity allows participants to teach one

another what they have learned by answering questions on key concepts covered throughout the training program. Place participants in groups of four and have everyone answer the question revealed on the slide when it is their turn. Each breakout group should have enough slides, one question each, for each person to answer at least one question. If there is more time, allow each person to answer two questions. The same questions can be used for all the groups and the time needed depends on how many questions they have to answer. To debrief the activity once all have returned, spend about 10 minutes asking where they struggled most, what was the easiest to answer, what they could not answer, and what they think will be most useful moving forward.

SETUP

Design needs ahead of time: Create a PowerPoint file with four to eight questions that ask participants to reflect on the main topics of the course. Include the questions in the participant manual for reference. Include a copy of each slide in the main deck for reference.

Before the activity begins:

Facilitator: Review the questions to ensure that all topics were covered in the training.

Producer: Prepare four breakout rooms. Ensure that the slides are loaded. Ensure that participants know how to move the slides forward to reveal the next question. Ensure breakouts are enabled. Ensure whiteboard tools are enabled in the breakouts. Provide guidance on the tools as needed.

THE ACTIVITY

SAY	DO
Facilitator: "To review the topics covered today, let's spend some time answering a few questions with one another in small groups. You'll be working in teams of four to teach one another what you have learned by answering the question you pull from a jar—that is, the question that comes up on the slide when it is your turn."	*Producer:* Ensure that all breakout rooms have the PowerPoint file with the questions already loaded. (Or if using WebEx, ready to be loaded quickly.) Divide participants into four groups. Start the breakouts that have already been prepared in advance. When one minute remains, send a "broadcast message" to the groups reminding them to pick a spokesperson and letting them know how much time remains so they can get ready to return. *Facilitator:* Allow teams to have at least 15 to 20 minutes to complete the activity. Visit each of the breakout groups to see how they are doing. Contribute ideas and help only if they ask or you think they will benefit from assistance.
Facilitator: "Now that we have all returned, let's review: Which question did you struggle with the most? Which one was the easiest to answer? Were there any you could not answer? What do you think will be the most useful answer moving forward?"	*Producer:* Using copies of the same slides the participants worked from, whiteboard the highlights from their answers while they take turns responding.

Transition after the activity:

Facilitator: "Now that you have reviewed the key topics from the program today by teaching each other, make a commitment to use these techniques in your upcoming encounters. Document your challenges and successes and we'll work through those in the next session. Until next time!"

SPICE IT UP WITH THESE ALTERNATIVES

- For an icebreaker, adjust the questions and run it at the beginning of a session. Here are some sample questions: "What famous person would you invite to dinner and why?" "If you could give your younger self some advice, what would it be?" "If you could be anywhere in the world right now, where would you be and why?" "If you could be any superhero, who would you choose and why?"
- Assign just one question to each team and ask them to deliver a full answer to the main group once everyone has reconvened.
- With no breakout groups, use the slides in the main deck and keep everyone together in the main room. (Prepare this as a backup if the breakout technology fails to work or if the platform does not have the breakout feature, like WebEx Meeting Center.)

A Geometric Close

Purpose: To debrief learning points at the end of a session, and help the participants define action items as a result of what they learned.

Session format: Training

Audience: Any training audience in which the reflective questions involved would be relevant

Number of participants: 5 to 16

Time: 10 minutes

Materials: PowerPoint file

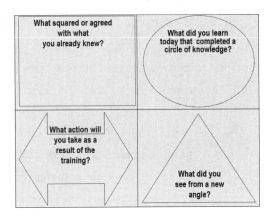

Features used: Share PowerPoint presentation, Whiteboard tools, Audio unmuted

---

Backstory

One of the first people to inspire me to write this book was Michelle St. Pierre. She shared this activity with me during one of the online training events I was conducting with her company at the time. Thanks, Michelle!

Note: A Geometric Close is adapted from *50 Creative Training Closers: Innovative Ways to End Your Training with IMPACT!* by Bob Pike and Lynn Solem (Wiley, 1998).

Description: This A Geometric Close activity works best with 5 to 16 participants, as you may run out of whiteboarding real estate on the screen. This activity helps manage the attendees who say they have not learned anything. The questions relate to the shapes on the slide, but are also thought-provoking and eye-opening:

- Square: "What squared or agreed with what you already knew?"
- Circle: "What did you learn today that completed a circle of knowledge?"
- Triangle: "What did you see from a new angle?"
- Arrow: "What action will you take as a result of the training?"

SETUP

Design needs ahead of time: Create a slide with the shapes like the example here.

Before the activity begins:

Producer: Ensure that whiteboard tools are enabled. Provide guidance on the tools if needed.

THE ACTIVITY

SAY	DO
Facilitator: "We're going to review today's session. On the whiteboard I've loaded four rectangles—each one has a shape inside of it. In the first rectangle, there is a square. In it, tell us what squared or agreed with what you already knew. Moving clockwise, in the next rectangle, there is a circle. What did you learn today that completed a circle of knowledge? For the triangle, tell us what you saw from a new angle. And last, in the space with the arrow, share what direction you're going to go in—what action will you take as a result of the training? Committing to these actions is a huge part of your success in this class, so don't be shy! Go ahead and annotate now in the space provided; it's OK if you go outside of the lines a bit."	*Producer*: Enable whiteboard tools. *Facilitator*: Comment on the responses, encouraging participants to provide examples and details as appropriate.
Facilitator: "Now that we are at the end of the activity and the program as well, here is how you can save the whiteboard if you wish."	*Producer*: Guide participants to save the whiteboard.
Facilitator: "Also, write your action items down on page [X] of your participant manual. You are more likely to take that action if you write it down! In the next session, we will check in on your progress."	*Producer*: Indicate in the chat the relevant page number.

Transition after the activity:

Facilitator: "Now that you have documented your action items, let's review what you can expect in the week to come, before we meet for the next session."

SPICE IT UP WITH THIS ALTERNATIVE

If it's a larger group and there's no need to capture action items, have each person only choose one shape to respond in, rather than responding in all four.

Word Search: Explain Yourself

Purpose: To reinforce for participants what they have learned by focusing on key words from the programs.

Session format: Training

Audience: Any training program in which there were numerous new words introduced or keywords used frequently

Number of participants: 5 to 16

Time: 10 minutes

Materials: A PowerPoint file

Features used: Share a PowerPoint presentation, Whiteboard tools, Audio

Description: A word search activity is simple to create, but determining how to use it can be challenging. In Word Search: Explain Yourself, participants use the annotation tools to circle or highlight the words they find, but they also explain how those words arose in the training. Have participants choose a color to circle or highlight to make it clear who found what word. Let each of them find at least one word and then start to call on them, one at a time, to explain how the word they found was important in the program. Participants will have fun with this, using their drawing tools to stay engaged and their memory and communication skills to recall what they have learned. There are websites with tools to create word searches, such as http://puzzlemaker.discoveryeducation .com/WordSearchSetupForm.asp.

SETUP

Design needs ahead of time: Create a puzzle and copy a version of it into the program's slide deck.

Before the activity begins:

Facilitator: Try the activity. Prepare an example to share with the group so they know how to perform the activity when it is their turn.

Producer: Ensure that whiteboard tools are enabled. Provide guidance on the tools as needed.

THE ACTIVITY

SAY	DO
Facilitator: "On the slide is a word search full of many of the terms and concepts we discussed and learned today. Choose a color from the whiteboard color palette and claim it as your own. Use that color to circle the words you locate, and then take a moment to think about that word and how it came up in our program today. I'll ask each of you to provide an example or to explain what we learned about that word once we all have found at least one."	*Producer:* Enable whiteboard tools. *Facilitator:* Give them a few minutes to find some; once you see that each person has found at least one word, begin to ask them to explain.
Facilitator: "It looks like each of you have found at least one. Let's take turns explaining what we have located and how it was addressed today. So, what did you find and what did we learn about it, *[Name]*?"	*Facilitator:* Ask each person to share and then wrap up. *Producer:* Help the facilitator keep track of how much time is left in the program so she ends on time.

Transition after the activity:

Facilitator: "I'm sure you agree that was a fun way to review and reinforce what we learned today! Thank you! Let's discuss what's next and what you can expect to have to complete before our next session."

SPICE IT UP WITH THIS ALTERNATIVE

Do not include the words to find on the list. This makes it more challenging, as participants need to think about possible relevant words from the program to look for.

A Call to Action

Purpose: To encourage participants to take action by chatting about what they will do after the live online event.

Session format: Training, Webinar, Meeting

Audience: Any that leaves a live online event with actions they need to take.

Number of participants: 5 to 16

Time: 5 to 10 minutes

Materials: 2 PowerPoint files/slides

Features used: Share a PowerPoint presentation, Chat, Audio

Description: This A Call to Action activity is perfect for the end of a live online event. It asks participants: "What will you do now that you have learned, heard, experienced, and seen this today?" Use one slide to make a strong point with the question itself and then move to a chat (or whitespace) to respond. If using chat in Adobe Connect, consider having a chat area dedicated just to this question. This makes it easy to save and refer back to for reports and follow up. Ask specific questions on their individual progress based on the saved responses.

Once participants have responded, move to the second slide with an inspirational quote and image. They have written their idea, and this slide helps encourage them to succeed. An inspirational quote can be simple and powerful, such as this one from Franklin D. Roosevelt: "Happiness lies in the joy of the achievement, and the thrill of the creative effort."

SETUP

Design needs ahead of time: Create one slide with the question in the center, in bold, in order to make an impact. Create a second slide for the inspirational quote and image.

Before the activity begins:

Facilitator: Clarify the reason why the quote and image were selected for the ending. Relate it to the learning and be specific with the action the participants are being encouraged to take.

Producer: Ensure that the chat tools are enabled.

THE ACTIVITY

SAY	DO
Facilitator: "We have discussed *[topic of your event]* today. Take a moment to think about what has really stood out for you; what really resonated and could be implemented right away. Which actions will you take first?"	*Facilitator:* Move to the new location (layout) where the chat is prepared for the participants to respond to your question.
Facilitator: "Take a moment now to write your response in the chat space provided. We'll be quiet on the audio for the next couple of minutes while each of you is thinking and typing."	*Facilitator and Producer:* Be sure to allow time for participants to think. Avoid the urge to comment on the first one that comes through.
Facilitator: "It's been a few minutes now and everyone has replied. Let's take a moment to read through each other's responses and comment on them."	*Facilitator:* Debrief with questions that you think are most appropriate, paying close attention to time so that you end on time.
Facilitator: "Thank you all for sharing your commitments and actions."	*Facilitator:* Move to the final slide and read the quote or tell a story. Relate it to the purpose of the session with a concise statement.

Transition after the activity:

Facilitator: "Now that you have each made your commitments to action, let's see what we can expect in our next session."

A Commitment Makes an Impact

Purpose: To close a session by having participants reflect on how they will use what they've
learned, what actions they will take, and the
effect the activity will have.

Session format: Training, Webinar

Audience: Any in which reflecting on the
learning event would be effective to aid in
learning transfer.

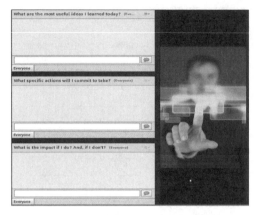

Number of participants: Unlimited

Time: 5 to 10 minutes

Materials: 3 questions, 1 image

Features used: Share an image, Chat

Description: This A Commitment Makes an Impact activity is a simple yet very effective
way to close an online session, no matter how many people are in attendance—whether it's
a 20-person training event or a 500-person webinar. It provides specific guidance on what
participants should be thinking about at the end of the session. Ask three questions—for
example, "What are the most useful ideas you learned today?", "What specific actions will
you commit to take?", and "What is the impact if you do and what is the impact if you do
not?" Participants will respond to the questions, one at a time, in the chat.

In a training event, call on participants to comment on their responses to the questions, further explaining what they meant. Participants can be encouraged to respond to
one another and comment, or perhaps even add to their own responses after hearing from
others. In a webinar, use the chat to comment on some of the participants' responses and
make general comments about the reflections as a whole. Chatting something as specific
as these three answers helps people commit to the action and really think about the difference it can make if they choose to act.

SETUP

Design needs ahead of time: Separate the questions in three chat pods (if using a platform that uses pods). Post the questions in the chat one at a time, have them respond to one question at a time, and separate the responses with textual line breaks like "*********" (if using a platform with only one main chat). This will make it easier to identify the different questions and answer segments on a saved chat file following the event.

Before the activity begins:

Producer: Ensure that chat tools are enabled. Prepare to copy the questions into the chat if necessary.

THE ACTIVITY

SAY	DO
Facilitator: "As we come to a close today, let's take the remaining time to reflect upon what we learned and what we will do next. On the screen are three questions for you to respond to: • "What are the most useful ideas I learned today?" • "What specific actions will I commit to take?" • "What is the impact if I do and what is the impact if I do not?" Take a few minutes to think about each and respond in the appropriate chat box.	*Facilitator*: In a training event, read each participant's responses, and begin to prepare questions for the debriefing. In a webinar, read as many responses as you can, but do not expect to be able to read all of them. Note common themes, and prepare to generally comment when the time comes to end the program. Do not comment out loud on the audio as soon as the first response comes through. Stay quiet for a few minutes, until everyone has had a chance to reply.

Transition after the activity:

Facilitator: "We have learned a lot today, committed to actions, and considered the impact of those actions, including the impact if we do not act. Now it is time to go and do it!"

Birds Flock Together

Purpose: To document the teamwork arising from your online event, and to provide a visual of each individual's contribution.

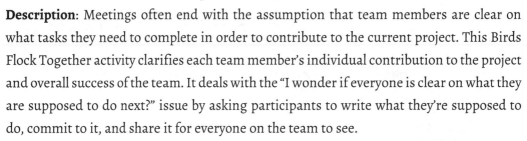

Session format: Meeting

Audience: A project team

Number of participants: 5 to 16

Time: 10 minutes

Materials: A PowerPoint file

Features used: Share PowerPoint presentation, Whiteboard, Audio

Description: Meetings often end with the assumption that team members are clear on what tasks they need to complete in order to contribute to the current project. This Birds Flock Together activity clarifies each team member's individual contribution to the project and overall success of the team. It deals with the "I wonder if everyone is clear on what they are supposed to do next?" issue by asking participants to write what they're supposed to do, commit to it, and share it for everyone on the team to see.

In the example here, the formation symbolizes the team, and the birds represent each individual's contribution to the team. Having team members type their action item next to a bird creates a visual that can be saved for reference and follow-up after the meeting. It also serves as a commitment to the task, providing an opportunity for anyone who needs to ask clarifying questions the chance to do it once they see what each person is actually working on.

SETUP

Design needs ahead of time: Prepare a slide with an image of birds flying in formation like the one above. Be sure there is enough room to whiteboard on top of the image, near each bird.

Before the activity begins:

Facilitator: Clarify that each person knows how to use the whiteboarding tools.

Producer: Ensure that whiteboard tools are enabled. Provide guidance on the tools as needed.

THE ACTIVITY

SAY	DO
Facilitator: "We have many tasks to do in order for this project to be completed. We all need to come together to make it happen! We are a team, each playing a vital role to the success of this project. Take a moment now to add your task to a bird. If you have more than one, use an additional bird. Type your name after each one. Let's see how we all bring this team together."	*Producer:* Assist with the whiteboard tools as necessary.
Facilitator: "Wow! We have a lot to do, but it's now clearer and we can see how we all contribute. Who has the first question on the tasks you see listed?"	*Facilitator:* Conduct a discussion, answering questions, clarifying tasks and roles, and making plans for the next meeting. *Producer:* Save the file and distribute it to the team members.

Transition after the activity:

Facilitator: "All right, we are clear! We've saved the file and will share it with each of you via email. Stay connected to each other, keep me updated on progress, and we'll all report back at next week's check-in meeting. Thank you!"

SPICE IT UP WITH THIS ALTERNATIVE

Use any image suitable for the team—have participants write in where they "fit" within that image. Emphasize how when everyone is together, it completes the image.

Conclusion

Not leaving enough time to properly close an online event is one of the biggest mistakes facilitators can make. Managing time requires that you start on time, control tangents that arise, and watch the clock. A great close means ending with engagement and impact, and a well-designed activity is a great way to get this result.

8

Gather Together:
Celebrations and Parties

· ·

Recognizing important milestones—such as graduations, retirements, engagements, anniversaries, weddings, and the birth of children—in the lives of the people on virtual teams is a powerful way to engage the participants. Holidays and birthdays provide themed opportunities to throw "virtual celebrations."

Unique and wonderful online parties can take a tremendous amount of preparation and planning, and in some cases, an element of surprise. This chapter outlines the specifics of several activities that can be used for a holiday party and a farewell celebration. It also includes a step-by-step plan for a surprise baby shower that will thrill any parent. Any of these activities could be altered and used for other types of events

Backstory

To this day, when I hear the song "Firework" by Katy Perry, feelings of joy come over me. I also get a little emotional because it was the song my former team at InSync Training played for me in my virtual going away party. We celebrated six years of working with these wonderful people entirely online, some of which I had never met in person but with whom I nonetheless felt very close. We played games, shared stories, remembered funny times and accomplishments, and we said good-bye to one another all using an online meeting tool. It meant the world to me.

like birthdays and anniversaries. Simply adjust the topic, arrange the images, and change the games.

These activities will inspire the online participants and make them feel honored to have been part of building and maintaining a virtual team. Enjoy, create, and celebrate!

Happy Holidays!

Purpose: To celebrate a holiday

Session format: Party

Audience: Virtual teams

Number of participants: Up to 20

Time: 10 minutes

Materials: A slide

Features used: Slide used for whiteboarding, Presenter rights to share, Annotation tools, Audio, Chat, Webcams

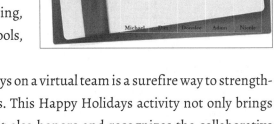

Description: Gathering together for holidays on a virtual team is a surefire way to strengthen the relationships of the team members. This Happy Holidays activity not only brings a virtual team together to celebrate, but it also honors and recognizes the collaborative nature of the team.

Backstory

This activity was developed from an idea one of the instructional designers at Dale Carnegie Digital, Nan Drake, had after she threw this celebration with her in-person team the year before. It is special because it also includes a donation to a children's charity of each team member's choice instead of burdening each team member with shipping a gift across the country or world.

SETUP

Design needs ahead of time: Create a slide with two tables, stacked on top of each other. Design the bottom table with a grid but no names. Animate the top table to fly in on a click with the names of the team members. This works best if the top table has no background so that the names seem to just appear when the table flies in. Names are selected after participants type their names in empty boxes on the bottom table, so that when the next slide or page up button is pressed, the top table flies in, revealing whom each participant has drawn.

Before the activity begins:

Facilitator: Confirm that the slide is working and has all team members' names added. For the second meeting, confirm all team members' slides have already been loaded before the meeting.

Producer: Ensure that the slide is loaded. Prepare to pass presenter rights as needed.

THE ACTIVITY

Step 1: Draw names using the stacked tables

Draw names using the slide with two tables, stacked on top of one another and animated to reveal the second table only after everyone has typed their name on the first one. This creates an element of surprise. If participants draw their own name, simply make a quick rearrangement.

Step 2: The Assignment

Once names are drawn, the fun really begins. Participants are asked to purchase a gift for the person they were assigned that they think the person would have loved as a child. Gather the team in another meeting a week later to reveal what the participants purchased and to share a little about themselves at the same time. To purchase a gift for the person they had drawn, have participants make an effort to reach out to that person to get to know them. The secret part is not whom they drew, but rather the gift they chose. At the end, donate the gifts to a local children's charity.

Once the gifts have been purchased, have each participant prepare a slide to bring to the party. The slide should contain three pictures: a picture of the gift, a picture of the person as a child, and a picture of the person today. Let participants know they'll be gathering in an online session to share their slides.

Step 3: The Party

The week leading up to the party, reach out to the team members and ensure that everyone is ready to upload their slide for the party. Open the party 30 minutes early and ask the team members to email their prepared slides. Upload them in share pods and give team members Presenter rights when it is their turn to reveal. Begin with a volunteer and proceed with the person who had drawn the volunteer's name so the next gift follows the viewing of that person's picture as a child on the previous slide.

Have team members reveal their slides, remind everyone whose name they had drawn, wait for the laughter to die down, describe why they had chosen that gift (if necessary), and then let the person receiving it comment and give thanks. After that, have the team member reveal the other two pictures, which will help team members get to know one another and see what everyone looked like as a child.

This activity can be so much fun, laughter will be heard throughout the Internet. The party will be talked about for years to come and hopefully will become an annual tradition.

Bon Voyage! Farewell Card

Purpose: To celebrate a team member who is leaving for a new job or retirement.

Session format: Party

Audience: Virtual team

Number of participants: Up to 20

Time: 5 to 10 minutes

Materials: A slide

Features used: Share slide, Whiteboard and annotation tools

Description: In many organizations and departments, when a long-time colleague is retiring or moving on to a new job, someone buys or creates a farewell card for them. The same can be done for members of virtual teams. Simply load the "card" into the virtual meeting room in advance, giving all team members access to sign it throughout the week (or at least a few days prior). Then reveal it to the guest of honor on the day of the scheduled going-away party. Typically not everyone will be able to attend the party, so it will be nice that each person had a chance to sign and leave a message on the card throughout the week. The recipient will no doubt be very touched by this gesture. And be sure to take a screenshot of the card to share for a lasting memory.

SETUP

Design needs ahead of time: Create a slide with plenty of space for team members to leave messages.

Before the party begins:

Facilitator: Load the slide (card) and then let people join the party early to sign the card.

Producer: Ensure that the slide (card) is loaded. Enable whiteboard and annotation tools.

THE ACTIVITY

Step 1: Sign the card in advance.

Allow team members to sign the card, using whiteboard tools, ahead of time. This requires opening the room early or periodically throughout the time leading up to the party.

Step 2: Present the card at the party.

Once the party begins and the guest of honor has arrived, reveal the card and allow her time to read it. Be sure to take a screenshot to save a copy for her.

Bon Voyage! We'll Miss You

Purpose: To celebrate a team member who is leaving for a new job or retirement.

Session format: Party

Audience: Virtual team

Number of participants: Up to 20

Time: 5 to 10 minutes

Materials: A slide

Features used: Share slides, Whiteboard and annotation tools, Chat

Description: A Bon Voyage! online party can be an effective and fun way to thank an individual for his contributions to the team and do some team building (for those still on the team). This activity can take many forms, but asking everyone to share some memories or what they will miss most about the individual, and then giving a team leader a chance to say something more formal, is usually sufficient and powerful.

SETUP

Design needs ahead of time: Create a few slides indicating "well wishes" and some questions for the chat—for example, "What will you miss most about working with [name]?" and "Share your fondest memory of working with [name]?" Develop a second slide to use as a visual for a formal thank you for the individual's contribution to the team.

Before the party begins:

Facilitator: Load the slides, prepare the chat questions/pods.

Producer: Ensure that the slide (card) is loaded. Enable whiteboard and annotation tools. Enable public chat.

THE ACTIVITY

Step 1: Fill in the chat responses.

Create two chat pods (if using Adobe Connect) or use the main chat (if using another online meeting tool). Have people respond to the questions either before the party begins or during. It is a nice way to keep everyone active throughout the party. Periodically check in to see what has been added and perhaps request that some people read their entries out loud.

Step 2: Thank you, well wishes, don't be a stranger.

Display the additional slide that provides a visual for the formal thank you for the individual's contributions to the team. Have a manager or other leader give a short speech honoring the person and his accomplishments.

Bon Voyage! Curtain Call

Purpose: To celebrate a team member who is leaving for a new job or retirement.

Session format: Party

Audience: Virtual team

Number of participants: Up to 20

Time: 5 to 10 minutes

Materials: A slide

Features used: Webcam

Description: In the theater, a curtain call occurs at the end of a performance when individuals return to the stage to be recognized by the audience for their performance. In a Bon Voyage! virtual celebration, the webcam positioned on top of a cleverly designed slide is used as a final curtain call for the team to recognize and honor the person who is leaving. Have the guest of honor appear on to the webcam first. Each team member can then take a turn joining her on the webcam and sharing how much they have enjoyed working with her. Other team members may choose to tell a story or say a simple thank you.

Backstory

When we did this with one of our team members, it was very special and quite emotional. It affected our team in a wonderful way and we continue to find ways to use the webcam to build our team relationships.

SETUP

Design needs ahead of time: Create a slide with a curtain around the edges and space in the middle to position the webcam.

Before the party begins:

Facilitator: Load the slide. Prepare the webcam.

Producer: Ensure that the slide is loaded. Enable webcam rights.

THE ACTIVITY

Step 1: View the curtain.

Move to the slide with the curtain and position the webcam in the middle. Ask the guest of honor to come onto the webcam along with each team member as they take their turn to share a story. Have two people on the webcam at a time and take turns until each team member is done.

Step 2: Cheers!

Once everyone is done and sufficiently emotional, have a manager or team lead make a toast. For example, our operations manager at Dale Carnegie Digital, Cliff Heckman, not only did this, but he also sang "Ain't No Sunshine When You're Gone" over the phone. It was lovely and memorable.

Step-by-Step Guide to a Surprise Virtual Baby Shower

A baby shower is a wonderful way to celebrate the pending or recent birth of a child. But sometimes getting together in person with everyone is just not practical. Rather than not hold the event at all, consider a virtual baby shower. Better yet, making it a complete surprise for the mother adds an extra layer of fun and impact.

Backstory

I'd like to thank Elizabeth Rigney, virtual facilitator and producer at EJR Consulting, for her expert party planning skills, creative ideas for games, technical skill, and hours of dedication as we hosted countless celebratory events like this baby shower over the years. Without her there it would not have been nearly as fun or effective enough to get feedback like this from one of the moms-to-be, Courtney: "When I talk about how much generosity I was showered with before the birth of my first baby I always mention the online one. I had a total of five baby showers and one of them happened to be virtual."

STEP 1

Arrange a "staff meeting" or appropriate pretense for a gathering, complete with a fake agenda sent out to each person before the meeting. Prepare a slide that will be the first slide seen when each person joins the online meeting. After everyone joins and gets connected to the meeting, read through the agenda and confirm everyone is on the same page by asking everyone to "click a green check" to agree with the agenda.

STAFF MEETING AGENDA
- Project Updates
- Process Changes
- Company Updates
- Q&A

STEP 2

Reveal the surprise with a slide devoted to the guest of honor. Decorate it with images—for example, with the guest of honor's photo and her due date. Or open the party

SuRpRiSe!
A Virtual BABY Shower!

with the typical "surprise!" from everyone and then go on to tell a story that makes everyone laugh and enjoy the moment.

STEP 3

Play some games! Here are some classic baby shower games translated to the online environment. It might be surprising how easy they are to play and also how similar they are to playing in person.

Concentration

Purpose: To have fun testing your memory.

Session format: Party

Audience: Baby shower

Number of participants: Unlimited

Time: 5 minutes

Materials: 3 slides

Features used: Share slide, Whiteboard

Description: In person, this game is played by filling up a tray with as many baby items that can fit on it. Next, a person walks around the room giving each participant a minute or two to study the items. After each person has had a moment to review the items, they are taken from the room and everyone writes down what they remember. The winner gets a prize and the mom-to-be gets all the items.

Online, this works by just creating a few slides: one to explain the game, one with the items, and a third to write answers. Show the slide with the items for one to two minutes, and then forward to the next slide and try to name all the items. No cheating by taking a screenshot.

ACTIVITY DETAILS

Design needs ahead of time: Create a title slide to introduce the game and explain how to play, a slide full of as many baby items as possible, and a slide with space to type what items participants recall seeing.

Before the activity begins:

Producer: Ensure that the slides are loaded. Enable the whiteboard tools. Provide whiteboard tool assistance if needed.

What the Heck Is It?

Purpose: To test your product identification skills.

Session format: Party

Audience: Baby shower

Number of participants: Unlimited

Time: 5 minutes

Materials: 2 slides

Features used: Share slide, Whiteboard tools

Description: This game is always a big hit simply because there is no shortage of unusual baby supplies available to new parents today. Even funnier is that many of them look like they are from another universe because they are so odd! Search the Internet for baby supplies or take pictures of items at a local baby supply store. Leave space on the slide for labeling, and

simply sit back and enjoy as the mom-to-be studies the images and perhaps becomes a little worried about what more she needs to learn about taking care of a baby. After a few moments, allow the other participants to be of assistance. Be sure to keep a key to all the items, because you may forget or not know what each item is.

ACTIVITY DETAILS

Design needs ahead of time: Create a title slide to introduce the game and explain how to play and a slide with odd baby supplies and space for labeling them.

Before the activity begins:

Producer: Ensure that the slides are loaded. Enable the whiteboard tools. Provide whiteboard tool assistance if needed.

Celebrity Name Game

Purpose: To test team members' Hollywood knowledge.

Session format: Party

Audience: Baby shower

Number of participants: Unlimited

Time: 5 minutes

Materials: A slide

Features used: Share slide, Whiteboard

Description: How much do you pay attention to the news about Hollywood stars? It can be a fun activity to test knowledge in this area. All you need to do is conduct an Internet search on movie stars and their children's names. Create a two column slide with the stars on the left and their children's names on the right. Enable the whiteboard tools and start matching. Use letters and fill-in-the-blanks. This activity is fun and quick, and is sure to get everyone laughing at some of the very interesting and unusual names.

Tip: Be sure to have an answer key available just in case.

ACTIVITY DETAILS

Design needs ahead of time: Conduct research on the Internet and create a two-column slide with the names of the parents on one side and the children on the other (in jumbled order of course).

Before the activity begins:

Producer: Ensure the slides are loaded. Enable the whiteboard tools. Provide whiteboard tool assistance if needed.

The ABCs of Baby

Purpose: To see how many items you can name for each selected letter.

Session format: Party

Audience: Baby shower

Number of participants: Unlimited

Time: 5 minutes

Materials: A slide

Features used: Share slide, Whiteboard

	Toys	Boys Names	Girls Names	Clothing	Food
S					
T					
O					
R					
K					

Description: Online party attendees will have a wonderful time filling out a table like the example here. At an in-person baby shower, a game like this is usually played individually. A virtual baby shower offers an opportunity for collaboration; participants work together as a team to fill it in and laugh along the way. This game is perhaps best played toward the end of the party and works nicely to segue into potential names for the child (if the mom-to-be is open to doing so) or questions she may have about the best food or toys to get at certain ages. Simple and fun.

ACTIVITY DETAILS

Design needs ahead of time: Create a slide with a table on it: the first row should have "Boys Names," "Girls Names," "Toys," and "Food" as column headings. Fill the cells in the column on the left with "baby" and the name of the mom-to-be.

Before the activity begins:

Producer: Ensure the slide is loaded. Enable the whiteboard tools. Provide whiteboard tool assistance if needed.

Continuing the Step-by-Step Guide to a Surprise Virtual Baby Shower

STEP 4

Share some insights and wisdom. Ask the members of the team to share their best practices on being a parent. Gather the insights on one slide and share it during the meeting. Here is an example, including the last bit of advice: "Don't listen to any of this. You will know your baby best and what is best for you baby!"

STEP 5

Offer best wishes and congratulations to the happy couple. Create a slide with a picture of the parents-to-be, leaving space for all the participants to sign it, like a card.

STEP 6

Send a gift. Everyone can contribute and the gift can be ordered and sent directly to the new mom. It could be a gift for the baby—or the mother.

Conclusion

Events such as holidays, birthdays, graduations, retirements, engagements, anniversaries, weddings, and upcoming births can all be celebrated online and can provide a powerful way to engage members of a virtual team. Such virtual celebrations require preparation and planning, but the examples provided in this chapter are specific approaches that have been proven to get great results. Vary the details as needed, and then celebrate—online!

9

The Next Level: Advanced Features and Fine-Tuning

. . . .

Once the basic functions and features of the online event platform have been mastered, the next step is to learn the secrets for using more advanced tools such as webcams and multimedia. This also includes learning the tricks to managing breakouts and helping participants work in small groups so that these activities don't fail due to technology glitches and misunderstandings.

Webcams, multimedia files, and breakouts are not required to run a successful virtual event. In fact, think about the last webinar or online training you attended. Did the organizers introduce themselves through their webcams or use any of those features to deliver the presentation or to conduct an activity? Perhaps they did; if they didn't, that's because these extra features are beyond the basics and can enhance participant engagement when used properly. They can also disrupt the engagement, or even take down the entire event should the technology fail to work as expected.

These features require extra technical knowledge, and sometimes involve specific computer requirements or software to ensure that the features work as they are designed. For webcams and multimedia use, the technology goes beyond connecting and sharing a presentation: they involve the computer's audio and video components, such as adjusting the controls of the output and input in the sound settings. Also important is knowing what type of computers and operating systems the participants will be using to join the event. PC settings are different from those of a Mac, and the mobile application settings are different on the Apple "i" products from those on Android-based products. The output from a PC webcam will likely look different from a Mac webcam. And the way it displays to each participant depends on the participant's operating system and compatibility of the device. For instance, the breakout function (if the platform includes this feature) may work with a PC or a Mac, but not with mobile applications. While breakouts can be very engaging, they can quickly become confusing and even fail entirely if you don't know how to facilitate them, or how the platform works, or how many participants can use them.

In addition to all the technical details, how each of these features will be used needs to be accounted for during program design. Breakout activities require special attention and timing, so avoid trying them on the fly. Participants are easily lost and usually need directions for how to do the breakout activity in several ways: on the audio, on the slide, and printed in their manuals. Webcams take time to enable and then adjust. So when designing activities that use webcams, pay close attention to the timing involved so that each participant performs the activity as planned. And when you play audio and video files, plan for how long they are and for an appropriate debriefing afterward.

A little extra technical knowledge, some additional skill using the platform, and careful preparation and planning will go far in making these advanced features work in the online event. This chapter details exactly what is needed to take online events to the next level.

Webcams

Webcams are the most often used advanced feature. Most presenters use their embedded webcams, but because these webcams are not of high video quality, it may be wise to purchase an external webcam instead. Extra attention should be paid to the platform settings in order to use them effectively. Be sure to test the platform's speed and size settings and then view it from a second computer to ensure that the result meets the necessary quality standards. While webcams can be used to effectively communicate with and engage an online audience, they mostly underwhelm and unnecessarily overload the bandwidth. Here are five areas to consider when deciding whether to use a webcam.

1. **Engagement is in the eye—and ear—of the beholder.** Participants will form their own opinions on what will engage them, related to that topic, on that day, in that platform or space, and with that facilitator. Online training industry experts speak of participants having a moment of excitement when they realize a webcam is being used, but the interest often fades. Turning it on at key points can add context and interaction, without taking up bandwidth or using a tool just because it's available.

Backstory

Every time I present a webinar, I ask participants who come early if they would like to say hello on their webcams. Last year I delivered around 50 webinars. I can recall exactly two times when online learning participants agreed to do it. Most people did not have webcams and those who did, did not want to be seen in the event with other people they did not know.

I once conducted a test during which I planned to stay on the webcam the duration of the one-hour webinar. I memorized my key points and interactive moments, worked hard to look directly into the camera, warned participants I'd be looking at the chat at certain times instead of directly into the camera, and did my best to make it seem I was looking at them when they were responding to questions and comments made during the session. After 20 minutes they unanimously agreed that although they loved seeing me introduce myself on camera, they respectfully asked me to turn it off because it was distracting them from the topic of the program. I couldn't have been more pleased to turn it off so I could finally get to focus on *them* and their responses to the content and interaction, rather than whether I was looking into the camera properly.

2. **Use the right tool for the job.** Does the webcam support and drive the event's objectives and help the participants better understand what is being communicated? If the answer is yes, use the webcam; if the answer is unclear, don't until you find out. If a person needs to receive critical information from the presenter's face as the speaker looks into a webcam, webcams can be effective. In these cases, facilitators or presenters need to be great performers, modeling themselves after those who work in broadcasting. Replicating the idea of "looking" at others only occurs if everyone is on a webcam at the same time.

Backstory

A perfect example of the webcam being used properly to meet a learning objective was when the IT director taught our team how to use our new VoIP phones. He used the webcam to zoom in on the buttons on the actual phone. It was useful, more engaging, and clearer than a screenshot could have ever been. It was as though he was at our desks, all of us at the same time. A brilliant use of the platform's tool.

3. **Events with people who already know each other are different from public learning or client events.** Simply having participants who know each other on a personal level or at least work together is a game changer. Participants are not as nervous to be seen on camera when a relationship or common experience already exists. In these familial cases, the novelty of the webcam feature takes over, and seeing a colleague not seen in a while makes it an enjoyable experience. In this case, participants usually come on webcam together, thus taking the focus off any one person as they look and respond to each other instead.

   In recent online sales presentations, we have used the webcam to lighten up the tone of the call. People become more at ease (with their nonverbal body language) when talking to each other once they see each other on camera. People smile and then seem to really open up. But after saying hello on the webcams, they quickly want to get back to business and turn off the cameras so they can focus. For these calls, the cameras become distracting once the introductions have been conducted.

4. **A meeting, webinar, or learning event is not usually supposed to be about the facilitator, it is supposed to be about the participants and the content.** Seeing a facilitator on a webcam during a live online event tends to make it about the person delivering it and not the participants. Participants thus expect a performance that entertains or inspires. They don't necessarily learn something that they can then do, like using new software, implementing a new process, or trying a new technique. And this brings the discussion back to using the right tool for the job. If participants need to learn something that they need to do, use, implement, or try, then they need to be the ones doing, using, implementing, or trying while on the call or web event.

Here are some guidelines for when and how to use a webcam for online meetings, webinars, and training events.

- **Meetings**. First, get everyone connected to the meeting and then on the webcam. Warn participants in advance so that they are prepared to use their webcams. If using Adobe Connect, make a layout in which the webcam pod is the only pod. If using WebEx, change the view so you see everyone at once. While everyone is on the webcam together, use one of the icebreakers in this book to help everyone get to know each other. Take a moment to warm up the virtual team and watch how the communication easily flows. Turn them off to get focused on the meeting.

- **Webinars**. Ensure that the lighting is set, and look directly into the camera. Open the webinar with a smile and welcome everyone. After making contact with the participants, consider turning off the webcam until it would make an impact again, such as when reviewing the key points or calling participants to action at the end of the webinar.

- **Training events**. Introduce yourself, tell a story to let them get to know you, and then, if you have informed your participants to come webcam ready, allow them the same opportunity to introduce themselves and wave to one another. Use the webcams when it would benefit the participants to see each other; for example, communication skills training activities in customer service, or when viewing hardware and equipment, as in the example we stated above.

5. **Looking great on the webcam.** Here are some tips on how to dazzle while presenting over a webcam. Matthew Rolston provided tips on "How to Look Good on a Webcam" (available on YouTube, www.youtube.com/watch?v=FMex-9FyljU), and these are relevant for online presenters in the following ways:

- **Smile.** And the participants will smile too.

- **Pay attention to the lighting.** Do not be backlit, side-lit, or screen-lit. Follow the tips in the video to ensure that you have an appropriate glow to your lighting.

- **Adjust the webcam angle.** Position the lens equal to the hairline. There is no need to raise the computer the entire time, but pay close attention to your lens level when introducing yourself.

- **Create a professional background.** Keep it simple and clean, or participants will comment when the background is not appropriate. Adjust the background to establish credibility as an online professional.
- **Look at the participants, not yourself.** Don't treat the webcam as a mirror. Avoid looking at yourself, or at notes or a second monitor; look into the lens instead.

Make a point to look great on the webcam. The live online environment is very visual so this is one of the first places you can engage the participants.

Multimedia

Multimedia like audio and video clips are another way to mix things up and add an engaging element to online events. Here are 10 questions to answer in order to make sure everything is ready to go and to limit any problems that may arise.

1. **What multimedia formats are compatible with the platform?** As in, which files will actually play on the platform? For example, in Adobe Connect, to play an audio or video clip, simply use a share pod to load a file in one of these formats: SWF, FLV, MP3, MP4, or F4V.

2. **Can you send a link to a video posted on a website?** It would be so simple to just share the screen and navigate to a website where the video is posted and then just press "Play." The problem is that participants are not going to hear the video unless you hold your audio connection up to the computer. It will also be very choppy for them as the screen share tries to send the images to each of the participants. Not optimal. But what about instead sending the link to each participant? Check *Share > Web Content* in WebEx, and check the *Web Links* Pod in Adobe Connect. In other platforms check the available choices when sending a link with a video to participants.

3. **How do you load the audio or video file into the platform?** Instead of linking to a website to play a video, another option is to load a file from the computer into the platform. In Adobe Connect, a file loaded into a share pod can be controlled by the facilitators, and the sound will play from each participant's computer

speakers. In WebEx, load the multimedia file using *Share > Document* and it will appear as a separate tab at the top of the main content window. It will play and be heard on the participants' computers in much the same way as it is in Adobe Connect.

4. **What are the technical requirements for the participants?** When playing audio or video files, participants need to be able to hear and see them from their own connections to the event. What players will they need in order for the file to work? For example, .swf is a Flash file so participants will need Adobe Flash in order for it to work properly.

5. **What happens on the audio when you play the file?** Whether using VoIP or teleconference for the event, you will need to understand how the multimedia file will interact with the audio. Mute all participants before pressing the play button to ensure that the sound is nice and clear, and only playing from each participant's computer. Test this before the live event.

6. **Can you adjust the volume of the sound?** Does the platform allow for control over the volume of the file? If not, be sure to provide directions to participants that they may need to adjust the volume on their own computers in order to comfortably listen to it.

7. **Who can control the play, pause, and stop buttons?** Make sure it is clear who has control of the file. For example, in WebEx it is the presenter who controls the play, pause, and stop of a multimedia file.

8. **Does it get included on the recording?** Play the file while making a test recording. See if the multimedia clip gets recorded, and if it does, if the timing matches up to the file. If it does not and you plan to make a recording for viewing after the event, be sure to provide a link to the multimedia clip to those who are watching the recording in addition to the recording link. Such foresight goes a long way.

9. **Does the file stay in place if you change presenters?** Sometimes there may be many presenters, so make sure the clip is ready to play when it is your turn. In WebEx, if the presenter role is changed to someone who did not load the multimedia file, the file will not appear. Test the platform and make sure the desired file is available when needed.

10. **What is the backup plan if the file does not play?** If a participant cannot view or hear the file, what is the backup plan? Have a video file on a website as a backup and send the link in chat for separate viewing for anyone who needs it. For an audio file, provide a transcript of the text in the appendix of the handout so they can read it instead.

Breakouts

The key to facilitating successful breakout activities is clarity. Deliver clear and direct instructions to the participants, and be very clear on the step-by-step process yourself, including the technical aspects. Separate the activity and technical directions and start each instruction with an action verb, using as few words as possible. The participant manual can contain full sentences, but simple and direct slides are best kept to the key phrases. Treat them as "at a glance" summaries because participants should be able to glance at the slides while managing any concerns of having to work in a small group. Concerns arise because participants know they really have to pay attention in order to complete the assignment, and they are going to have to use the virtual meeting tool on their own. Participants have to pay attention to the activity directions, the page in the manual, the technical directions, their partners, how much time they have, and how to ask for help. That's a lot. Here's a three-step breakout process that will help keep the breakouts clear and concise and ensure that participants are engaged.

THREE-STEP BREAKOUT PROCESS

Plan to create a minimum of three slides for the main training file to clearly facilitate each breakout activity. For the actual activity, create a separate slide that restates the instructions and provides whiteboarding space to take notes. This separate slide should be loaded (or preloaded if the platform supports this) into each breakout room. The teams then have clear instructions on what to do and where to document their work. This is how to minimize confusion and keep participants from needing help as soon as they enter their breakout room.

Here are the three breakout slides, which represent the three breakout steps we include in our main training presentation.

Step 1. Introduce the breakout activity. Use the first slide to transition from where participants have been, where they are going, and how this activity will help them. This is also a good time to provide an example or a story to set the stage to prepare them to work on the activity together or on their own, until you join their breakout to check on them.

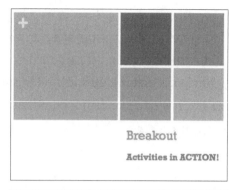

Step 2. Provide instructions for the breakout activity. Use the second slide to explain what the participants will be doing. But be sure to separate the activity instructions from the technical directions. Plan to deliver the activity instructions and ask for questions on the assignment and how to successfully complete it first. Once participants are ready to do the activity, they

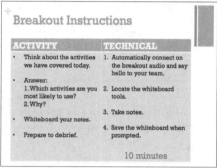

will be ready to listen to how they will get into the breakout and work together. Ask the producer to deliver the technical directions. Include a timing reminder on the slide and remember this slide is also for those who were not listening or had stepped away. They can quickly look at it and get up to speed on what to do next.

Step 3. Regroup and debrief. Prepare a third slide to welcome the teams back and possibly to use as a debrief whiteboard. Another option is to load the slides or materials they worked on in the groups and take turns displaying their work. Check the platform to see the easiest way to do this: it could be sharing a breakout share pod (Adobe Connect), sharing breakout content (WebEx Training Center), or passing the pres-

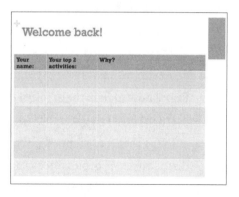

enter controls to the leader of the group and asking her to share her screen, one at a time.

10 THINGS TO WATCH OUT FOR IN BREAKOUTS

1. **Participants are not hanging on your every word.** To support the verbal directions, repeat them in the participant manual and simply state them on a slide.

2. **Don't assume the audio will automatically transfer into the breakout room.** Check it beforehand.

3. **If assigning a leader to the breakouts, contact him first.** Sometimes people walk away from their desks and cannot lead the breakout, leaving the other attendees waiting and wondering, unable to complete the activity.

4. **Participants often feel lost in a breakout.** Be very clear with the instructions, answering questions before launching the breakouts.

Backstory

"It's deadly to say, after you explain the breakout process, 'Do you understand?' The reason it's deadly is that they don't know what to ask, and then they get into the breakout room and are lost. It is much better to say, 'Who has the first question on what we are about to do?' This gives me time to answer any last minute questions as the producer gets ready to start the breakouts."

—Donalee Frary, live online trainer, Dale Carnegie Digital

5. **Check in on the participants.** Participants rarely know how to ask for help once they are in the breakout room, so it is important to check in on them.

6. **Know how to move between breakout rooms.** In addition to needing to check in on participants, it is satisfying to hear the teams working together.

7. **Know how to help them join a group after it has been started.** Sometimes participants arrive late to class, after participants have started the breakouts. Or perhaps they had stepped away when the breakout activity started. Be able to help them join their group once it has already formed.

8. **Breakout activities are not usually recorded.** Consider leaving one group in the main room to capture an example of a team working on the activity. But let them know they are the chosen ones.

9. **Send broadcast messages to the teams.** Use this feature to send time checks and reminders on directions like choosing a speaker to debrief.

10. **Leave time for a proper debriefing.** Don't end the breakouts and not set aside time to hear what each group learned, created, and enjoyed about working together. This can stifle the positive energy and engagement that was created by doing the breakout activity.

Conclusion

Webcams, multimedia files, and breakouts are not required to run a successful virtual event, but in some cases they can help take a good event and make it great. This chapter provided advanced guidance, best practices, and tips for using these online platform features for online activities. Armed with all the activities in this book and now this information on advanced platform features, there is nothing stopping you from creatively designing online events that will engage participants and get results.

10

Take Charge:
Create Your Own Activities

. . . .

So what's next? That's simple. Get out there and engage the participants: you can do it. This book has activities of all types to dramatically improve engagement levels in virtual training, meetings, and webinars. So when delivering live online events, remember these eight easy steps:

1. **Identify the goals.** Engaging, entertaining, and using all the platform features are not end goals of a live online event. Clearly identify the purpose of the live online meeting, webinar, or training program—and then determine how and where activities can help reach the goals.

2. **Identify the audience.** Some audiences will want to be highly engaged and thus will benefit from having a lot of fun in the live online event. Others, such as high-level leaders, will not want to do anything they perceive as wasting time. New hires are different from employees with 20 years' experience. And levels of comfort with technology range from the techno-elite to the techno-phobic. Know the audience as best you can to choose activities that are both appropriate and will optimize engagement.

3. **Identify the time constraints.** Time determines how many activities, and which ones, are appropriate for the live online event, whether the program is 45 minutes,

two hours, or spread over six weeks. Some activities take five minutes, some take 20 or more. This can make all the difference.

4. **Learn the platform—inside and out.** As noted in chapter 1, there simply is no substitute for knowing the platform very, very well, whether it's Adobe Connect, WebEx, or any of the many others available. As the facilitator, don't rely solely on the producer to help when disaster strikes—be just as skilled with the technology. As the program designer, know the features available inside and out. How else will you be able to design the best activities to achieve the goals of the event?

5. **Start with a welcome activity.** Set the tone for the live online event by engaging participants with activity right from the start. This lets them know they aren't attending yet another online lecture or boring online meeting where they can multitask and not be fully engaged.

6. **Break the ice.** Take the time to set the stage for the participants and help them get to know one another, you, and how the platform will be used throughout the session. Participants are often unsure of how to communicate, let alone how to use features like chatting and whiteboarding. The icebreaker establishes the type of interaction planned for them. It also gives everyone a chance to test the features and make sure they know how to use them to ask questions, gain feedback, and learn from you and one another.

7. **Select appropriate meeting, webinar, or training activities.** This book provides more than 50 activities from which to choose. Not all of them will fit with all event types and audiences. Make sure to mix it up over time, too. Don't use the same activity in every online meeting and don't start every online training session with the same icebreaker. And remember that in most cases you won't be running back-to-back activities throughout a program. Announcements need to be made; information needs to be conveyed; and facts, concepts, principles, processes, and procedures need to be taught. Some of this content is best delivered in a lecture-style format. But with ample activities to break it up, you now can limit the lecture to 5 to 10 minutes at a stretch—keeping everyone engaged, while sharpening the impact of the lecture segments.

8. **End with a closer activity.** Don't forget to end on time with a meaningful, memorable closing activity. The participants will be pleased to leave knowing how they will apply or use what they have learned. Be sure to wrap up a meeting efficiently, capturing action items, task owners, and next steps. For a webinar, call them to action and provide resources for further inquiry and information. For a training event, allow them an opportunity to reflect on the learning and how they can use it to make a difference.

This may seem like a lot to cover. But over time, if you run enough live online meetings, webinars, and training programs, you will find appropriate spots for all these activities.

And note that the eight easy steps—and the approach taken throughout this book—does not say, "Use chat in an activity," or "Use whiteboards in an activity," or "Use breakouts." It's critical to not let the technology drive your design decisions. Instead, use the features available to you creatively, but in ways that always further the goals and that are appropriate to the audience.

Create Your Own Activities

The activities in this book are just examples—ones we've tried and been successful with, ones that make us laugh, ones we know will engage any audience. But there are countless other activities for live online meetings, webinars, and training programs. Inspiration might come from anything and anywhere. The world abounds with resources for meeting, webinar, or training activities that could be adapted to fit an online need.

But perhaps the most fertile ground for new live online activities is the in-person activities you have seen or participated in during your careers or even school years. Think about successful activities in the many in-person meetings and in-person training programs you have been part of over the years. The trick is adapting them, or ones similar, to the live online environment. Asking three questions can make this process easier:

- What activities do you enjoy running during an in-person event?
- What is the goal of the activity? What is achieved once the activity is complete?
- What features in the online tool can help reach that goal?

Consider this example. In a virtual team meeting we wanted to run an improv activity that we had done in person many times before. The in-person activity is effective because team members hone their nonverbal communication skills by performing an action with an object and then passing it to a partner, who then also needs to use that object. But the actual objects are not used—it is all done by miming. So a person may mime reading a book and then hand the book over to a partner who then turns a few pages. The partner then mimes casting a fishing rod and passes it to another partner. And so on until each person has had a turn.

But how would this work online where team members are not together in person to hand off the object? First, determine which available platform features would best suit this activity—for example, a webcam and a note pod. Alert everyone beforehand that they will be using their webcams for the next team meeting. Prepare a note pod with a list of all team members so that they can follow an established order. Have every team member take a turn on the webcam and use an object. Ask them to then pass it to the next person on the list who has to guess what it is by miming their receiving of the object. This is how Mime It! was created. (See chapter 4 for a detailed breakdown of this activity.)

This example shows how an in-person activity can be easily molded for a live online event. The activity was done a little differently online and required learning and using some online features, but the end goal was the same: clearer communication among team members, without using words. So trust us, you can do it. All you need is a little imagination and ingenuity.

We'd love to hear of any great live online activities you come up with on your own, especially after you've used them successfully in your meeting, webinar, or training program. Connect with us on LinkedIn, and let us know if you would like to share an idea for an activity. And who knows, perhaps your activity will fit nicely (with your permission, of course) into a second, expanded edition of this book.

Photo Credits

About the Authors

KASSY LABORIE

kassy.laborie@dalecarnegie.com

Kassy LaBorie is an online synchronous facilitator, producer, instructional designer, and virtual training platform expert. She is also a frequent and popular speaker at ATD and other learning and development conferences and events.

In her role as director of live online training for Dale Carnegie Digital, Kassy leads the development of the live online training events focusing on program design, trainer and producer development, and overall participant experience. Prior to joining Dale Carnegie, Kassy held positions as a master trainer for InSync Training, where she delivered online programs using the many platforms available, and as a senior trainer at WebEx helping to build the WebEx University. She started her training career as a software trainer for ExecuTrain, which allowed her to develop the necessary technical agility to effortlessly run online events. Kassy also developed relevant skills from her acting experience in college and even the time she spent as a FedEx foot courier in San Francisco, which taught her to control her breathing when delivering packages, exactly what's needed when delivering events online.

Regarding this book, Kassy says: "All of these professional roles—plus a whole lot of yoga!—have shaped my life and enabled me to bring the ideas in this book to you. I have shared what you can do to lessen the tension and minimize the stress of engaging an online audience, and have fun at the same time. I look forward to hearing of your successes with virtual training, meetings, and webinars—so look me up at conferences or connect with me online!"

Follow Kassy on Twitter: http://twitter.com/Kassy_L
Get LinkedIn with Kassy: http://www.linkedin.com/in/kassylaborie

TOM STONE
tom.stone@dalecarnegie.com
Tom Stone has been in the learning and development field for more than 15 years. He currently serves as director of content strategy for Dale Carnegie Digital where he manages the digital instructional design team, and sets the product roadmap and strategy for their live online and self-paced programs. Prior to joining Dale Carnegie, he was with e-learning provider Element K and talent management software provider Taleo in such roles as senior instructional designer, manager of content development, and senior research analyst.

He is a frequent and popular speaker at ATD and other learning and development and broader human resources conferences and events. He has delivered more than 100 presentations, workshops, and panels on topics such as live online and self-paced e-learning, social learning, mobile learning, industry trends, and other talent management subjects.

It was through one of these events that he met Kassy LaBorie, and later joined the Dale Carnegie Digital team.

Regarding this book, Tom says: "After joining Dale Carnegie, I quickly realized how much expertise and passion Kassy had for Live Online training. So when she suggested that I join her as co-author on her book project with ATD, I didn't hesitate. After all, I've written hundreds of blog posts, whitepapers, and research briefs on a range of talent management subjects—so how difficult could it be? While it took a lot of time and dedicated effort, I believe we have produced a practical book full of creative and useful activities for the virtual classroom. Thanks again, Kassy, for the opportunity to join you on this journey."

Follow Tom on Twitter: http://twitter.com/ThomasStone
Get LinkedIn with Tom: http://www.linkedin.com/in/tomrstone

About Dale Carnegie Training

Dale Carnegie Training is driven by their belief that every individual has unique and untapped power to impact the world. Founded in 1912, Dale Carnegie is now a global professional development firm with 200 offices in 90 countries, and with thousands of certified trainers delivering programs in 35 languages. Millions have graduated from its flagship Dale Carnegie Course, which local offices offer along with a broad range of public and organizational training programs in leadership, personal effectiveness, presentation and communication skills, sales, and customer service.

Dale Carnegie Training also offers interactive and engaging learning experiences through Live Online (Virtual Classroom) training programs. Participants develop their skills and competency through hundreds of public and private virtual classroom sessions every month. These live programs range from 1-hour webinars to 3-hour and multi-session workshops and seminars, and include numerous activities like those found in this book to provide instruction, coaching, and collaboration in small groups. Blended programs are offered that can combine in-person training, live online training, and other resources, and Carnegie Cloud—the industry's first live online talent development subscription—provides organizations access to a prepaid schedule of programs that can be mapped to desired competency frameworks or role-based learning paths. And finally, Dale Carnegie's Virtual Training Services offerings, led by Kassy LaBorie, help organizations improve their own live online programs by improving the skills of their trainers, producers, and designers.

HOW TO PURCHASE ATD PRESS PUBLICATIONS

ATD Press publications are available worldwide in print and electronic format.

To place an order, please visit our online store: www.td.org/books.

Our publications are also available at select online and brick-and-mortar retailers.

Outside the United States, English-language ATD Press titles may be purchased through the following distributors:

United Kingdom, Continental Europe, the Middle East, North Africa, Central Asia, Australia, New Zealand, and Latin America
Eurospan Group
Phone: 44.1767.604.972
Fax: 44.1767.601.640
Email: eurospan@turpin-distribution.com
Website: www.eurospanbookstore.com

Asia
Cengage Learning Asia Pte. Ltd.
Phone: (65)6410-1200
Email: asia.info@cengage.com
Website: www.cengageasia.com

Nigeria
Paradise Bookshops
Phone: 08033075133
Email: paradisebookshops@gmail.com
Website: www.paradisebookshops.com

South Africa
Knowledge Resources
Phone: +27 (11) 706.6009
Fax: +27 (11) 706.1127
Email: sharon@knowres.co.za
Web: www.kr.co.za

For all other territories, customers may place their orders at the ATD online store: **www.td.org/books**.